BATH COLLEGE

# The Royal Crescent in Bath

# The Royal Crescent in Bath

## A fragment of English Life

## William Lowndes

THE REDCLIFFE PRESS

First published in 1981 by
Redcliffe Press Ltd,
14 Dowry Square, Bristol 8

ISBN 0 905459 34 2

Printed in Great Britain by
Burleigh Ltd, Bristol

# Contents

# Illustrations

# Foreword

The Royal Crescent was the finest architectural achievement to emerge from Bath's remarkable eighteenth-century building renaissance. The dramatic symmetry of its noble, semi-elliptical curve, and the uncomplicated dominance of its great columns, identify it unmistakably as a masterpiece; in the words of Jan Morris, it 'provides one of the happiest moments of European sightseeing'. Its character has not only been engendered by physical attributes. Its uniqueness as a terrace of domestic dwellings has been embellished by the men and women who have lived there during the last two centuries, and who have added vitality to its timeless appeal. Houses without people are moribund. They don't breathe, or mellow gently with age: they are stone structures, and little else.

This is a book about the Royal Crescent and the people who have lived there. During the eighteenth century, when Bath's fame was at its height, many of those people took houses for the season. Some were famous, some were merely notorious; but most of them were interesting. So, too, were many of those who bought houses, and occupied them continuously over a number of years. They made the Crescent live, they gave it warmth, and emphasised its unique identity; without them, its beauty would have been qualified by a rather cold austerity.

To the best of my knowledge, this is the first book to be written about John Wood's masterpiece. It eschews technical, architectural detail, and thus makes no claim to be comprehensive; but if it gives pleasure and information to some of the innumerable admirers of one of Europe's finest buildings, then its object will have been abundantly achieved.

Like all writers on Bath, I am greatly indebted to the staff of the city's reference library. The local collection housed there, is a splendid one, and my frequent requests for guides, directories, letters, diaries, microfilms, newspaper cuttings and general books were all dealt with promptly and most courteously. I would also like to acknowledge the help given to me by Mr R. Bryant, archivist to Bath Corporation; Mr P. V. Christensen, General Manager, the Royal Crescent Hotel; Mr Clifford Francis; Mr Martin Fisher and

*Foreword*

Miss A. Wellesley-Colley. And, less seriously, I owe a small vote of thanks to an old friend, Leslie Cannon, Chief Librarian of the London Borough of Barking, who suggested that the title of the book should be 'The Royal Crescent in Bath: Coronation Street with Culture'. Less inspired flashes of wit have achieved a measure of immortality.

Bath.                                                                          *William Lowndes*

May, 1981

# 1 The Building of the Crescent

The *Bath Chronicle* for Thursday, 21st May, 1767, had more than its usual share of varied news items. It reported, for example, that "the right honourable the Earl of Chatham is grown better of the gout, insomuch that his lordship took an airing to Northend last Saturday". On that same Saturday, sporting readers were informed, "the great match between King Herod and Ascham was ran at Newmarket, which was won with ease by the former. The odds at starting were six to four in favour of Ascham". And for housewives who were more concerned about the rising cost of food than the activities of politicians and racehorses, there was the heartening news that butter was selling at fourpence a pound, and pigeons at eighteen pence a dozen. Editorial priorities don't seem to have changed a great deal over the last two centuries.

In that same issue of the Chronicle there appeared a small item of local news that probably made little impact on the paper's readers at that time. It read "Tuesday last, the foundation stone was laid of the first house of the intended new building above the Circus, called the Crescent". It was a cryptic announcement, clearly not expected to awaken a great deal of interest: yet it heralded the start of an enterprise that was to enhance Bath's fame and architectural beauty very considerably, and ultimately to evoke admiration from every quarter of the globe. Masterpieces, however, are seldom recognised at birth. Perhaps we should be grateful to the Chronicle's editor for including even a muted report; after all, speculative building was rife at that time in Bath, and new buildings were changing the city's appearance radically each year.

The Circus was completed in 1769. It was the brain-child of John Wood the elder, a man whose architectural genius was primarily responsible for creating Bath's eighteenth-century elegance. He laid the foundation stone of the first house in February, 1754. Three months later he died and his son, another John Wood — and, like his father, a brilliant architect — saw the work through to completion.

It is interesting to read the comments in the *Gentleman's Magazine* for 7th February, 1754, concerning the foundation stone laying.

9

"The first stone of the building which is to be called the King's Circus, and which is to consist of 33 elegant houses,* was laid" the magazine reported. "It is to be a circular area of 318 feet diameter, surrounded by 3 equal and similar piles of building, in theatrical style†. In the centre is to be an equestrian statue of His Majesty, and three streets, 52 feet wide, are to lead to it, each terminated with a fine building. But the principal approach will be one of the streets called Barton Street, leading from Queen Square to the Circus . . ."

Barton Street eventually became Gay Street, renamed after a London surgeon called Robert Gay who owned the land on which it was built. The other streets leading into the Circus were Bennett Street and Brock Street. Bennett Street was named after a mayor of Bath who was in office in 1773; and Brock Street owes its name to Thomas Brock, a Cheshire man who was the younger Wood's brother-in-law.

The statue of George II, which Wood senior had planned for the centre of the Circus, never materialised. The area was cobbled at first, and an early engraving from a fan shows a reservoir in the centre; it was fed by two or three good springs, and supplied the neighbourhood with water for several years. Then, early in the nineteenth century, the five great plane trees, now such a dominant feature of the area, were planted. Many people believe that, because of their size, they considerably reduce the impact of Wood's architecture on the observer. Bryan Little, author of *The Building of Bath*, has no doubt about it at all. 'The trees should be literally extirpated' he says, 'if need be by dynamite, so that justice may be done to the work of Bath's architectural masters'. Another critic, a little less indignant perhaps, complained that 'You can't see the Wood for the trees'.

In the original conception of the Circus and its surroundings, Brock Street was intended to be short, and terminated by an

---

*The houses are numbered 1—30, with 29 house-doors on the actual Circus. The four remaining doors are on return frontages — two in Brock Street, and two in Bennett Street.

†Wood senior took the Colosseum in Rome as his model for the Circus. The Colosseum, of course, was oval in shape; but the three superimposed orders of classical architecture — Doric, Ionic and Corinthian — were notable features of both buildings.

impressive building. But the younger Wood had other ideas. The demand for houses was great, and was increasing: more and more visitors were coming to Bath, ready and anxious to take a house for the season. What simpler than to create a longer street in a fashionable area that was growing so rapidly?

He had another, and more significant reason, however, for lengthening Brock Street. At the western end of the street there was a large plot of gently sloping ground adjoining the Common. Wood saw this as the perfect site for an ambitious plan that had been exercising his mind for some time — a plan that involved the design and erection of a great crescent of houses in the Palladian style. Because the Common could never be built upon, his new houses would have an uninterrupted outlook down to the Bristol road and beyond; and they would very conveniently be linked to the Circus by an extended Brock Street.

So, with the scheme taking shape in his mind, Wood designed the houses in Brock Street with modest façades. Nothing grandiose, he argued, should distract people as they approached the new crescent; a gentle stroll from the Circus along a dignified, but unremarkable street — and then the breathtaking view of his Palladian master-piece would explode before their eyes. It was a masterly conception; and it is as valid today as it was more than two hundred years ago.

The conveyance of the ground was granted to Wood and Thomas Brock, his trustee, by the landlord, Sir Benet Garrard, in December, 1766, at a ground rent of £200 per annum. Work commenced early in 1767 and, as we have seen, the foundation stone of the first house was laid in May of that year. Several individual contractors and craftsmen worked independently on the houses. The conditions under which they were employed were simple and effective. Wood engaged them to carry out uniform exteriors, according to his plans, but gave them freedom to alter interiors to suit individual tenants.* The builders, having arranged with tenants to lease the houses for a term of years, then took their agreements to the bank, and had no difficulty in obtaining money to commence work.†

---

*In every contract Wood insisted that, when each house was finished, its builder undertook to 'cleanse and tone down the stone work on the outside . . . to the end no crack may appear, and the whole building may be of one colour'.
†See Appendix 2.

As a result of this individual contracting, the interiors of the houses were by no means uniform; some were given elaborately beautiful ceilings, and room sizes differed widely. But no variations in interior design were allowed to affect the main façade in any way. The same conditions did not, unfortunately, apply to the rear of the building, and even before the Victorians added bathrooms and other outhouses, it presented a distinctly untidy appearance. An eighteenth-century architectural quip summed it up beautifully: 'Queen Anne in front, Mary Ann behind'.

Inevitably, of course, there were recurring problems at each stage of the Crescent's construction. As late as November 1773, for example, the *Chronicle* was reporting that 'we have authority to say that all disputes with regard to the ground at the front of the Crescent, are amicably settled'. And there were fatal accidents, too. A young mason's labourer fell from the scaffolding of one of the houses in October 1769, and was so badly injured that he died almost immediately. And in August of the following year a builder named George Clements tumbled from an attic storey, and a large stone that he had helped to carry up literally fell with him, and crushed him to death.

But early in 1775, some eight years after the laying of the foundation stone of the first house, the great project was completed. It must have looked even more majestic than it does today, if only because of its comparative isolation. Marlborough Buildings, at the west end of the Crescent, were not to be erected until 1790; and with open land stretching before it, there was a splendid prospect down to the river, interrupted only by occasional trees and houses along the Bristol road. From down there, with the new stone glowing gently in the sunlight, it must have presented a brave sight indeed.

Wood's plan had envisaged thirty houses in an elliptical curve more than five hundred feet in length. The two end houses were given return frontages along the diameter of the ellipse — a feature that seems to give the whole conception a new dimension, particularly when one views it from the bottom of the lawn. The ground floor façades were simply designed. But the first and second floors were decorated with one hundred and fourteen Ionic columns over twenty feet high, with an entablature rising to an open balustrade at roof level. The central house, No 16, had paired columns and a rounded first-floor window. The whole design was uncomplicated and immediately pleasing to the eye. But critics were not wanting, by any means. The author of an early Bath guide, *The Stranger's Assistant and Guide for Bath*, published in 1773 (before the Crescent was completed) wrote: 'The wretched attempt to make a centre to the Crescent where none was necessary, is absurd and preposterous to a high degree. The pairing of the pillars is too small a difference to be noted in so large a building, as is the window intended to be the centre . . . Had the centre been desired, it would surely have been more eligible as a chapel for divine service . . .'. How shocked the scribe would have been had he known that, a little more than two hundred years later, the central house of the Crescent was to become part of a superbly equipped hotel!

Even that great architectural authority Nikolaus Pevsner, was mildly censorious. In his *Buildings of England* he discusses the Crescent and says 'Even so, one hundred columns, so closely set and so uniformly carried through, are majestic, they are splendid, but they are not domestic'.

Undomestic indeed they may be; but the fact remains that admiration and acclaim over the years have far exceeded criticism. Visitors in their hundreds stroll along Brock Street, either individually or in conducted parties; even a wagonette from the Bath Carriage Museum clatters by from time to time, full of enthusiasts, and drawn by a mettlesome white horse. Eventually they all reach the last short, rising stretch of cobbled roadway, and turn into the Crescent — and the huge sweep of the Palladian façade is suddenly, startlingly before them. Eyes widen, fingers point, cameras are levelled. To many, the splendid prospect is clearly an unexpected and stimulating surprise — and this is exactly what John Wood envisaged. What he must surely never have guessed is that his masterpiece would still be capable of making the same impact more than two hundred years later.

One small detail needs to be mentioned here. It is often said that, at the outset, Wood christened his masterpiece simply 'The Crescent', and that the adjective 'Royal' was added only towards the close of the eighteenth century, after the Duke of York had resided at Nos 1 and 16. But in a contract drawn up between Wood and a builder called Michael Hemmings, conveying the ground for the building of

No 7 in 1767, the following appears: 'John Wood shall, at the costs of the said Michael Hemmings, convey unto him and his heirs for ever, All that plott, piece or parcel of ground being part of the field commonly called the Hayes Lower Furlong in the said Parish of Walcot, fronting westwards to an open area called the Royall Crescent . . . and the said Michael Hemmings does agree to build one substantial house at the westward end of the said ground, according to the plans of the said John Wood'. From this it would appear that the name 'Royal Crescent' was envisaged from the outset.

*       *       *

It was Horace Walpole, I believe, who coined that felicitous word 'serendipity', and defined it as the delightful faculty of making pleasing and unexpected discoveries by accident. Serendip is the ancient name for Sri Lanka, and Walpole's inspiration came from the title of a fairy story, *The Three Princes of Serendip*: its heroes were always making happily unexpected discoveries.

I have never believed that I possessed a quality of serendipity; but when, some years ago, I was searching for accommodation in Bath, I had reason to qualify this view. I wished to rent a flat in the city, preferably in a Georgian house, and I visited a dozen or more estate agents without a vestige of success. Then, one day, I dropped into 'La Vendange', a delectable little wine bar in Margaret's Buildings, off Brock Street. The lady behind the bar was sociable, and enquired if I were on holiday. I told her the purpose of my visit. 'Try my landlord' she said, scribbling a telephone number on the edge of a paper napkin, 'I think he has a flat to rent in the Crescent'.

So, by a delightfully happy accident, I discovered the drawing-room of No 5, Royal Crescent. The flat itself occupied the first floor of the house, and the rooms at the rear — bedroom, bathroom and kitchen — were unremarkable. But the drawing-room was a delight. It was an immense room, at least fourteen feet high, with a superbly moulded ceiling and an impressively large marble fireplace. Its three huge windows overlooked Victoria Park and the south-west prospect of the city, and allowed the afternoon sun to flood the room with light and warmth. Its acoustics were superb, and my record player produced sounds that were almost ethereal. My books and pictures adorned the walls most suitably: it seemed as though they had known no other resting-place.

If I eulogise too much, I may, perhaps, be excused. It was the ceiling that transformed the room, and heightened the appearance of almost everything in it. It was a miracle of delicate plasterwork that drew the eye repeatedly, and made one almost literally gasp at the standard of craftsmanship that had produced it. In Walter Ison's admirable book on the Georgian buildings of Bath, there is a technically full description of this small domestic miracle that is perhaps worth repeating: 'The exquisitely refined plasterwork decorating this room reflects the influence of the Adam designers, Bonomi and Pergolesi. The frieze of wreathed honeysuckle ornaments alternating with candelabrum is surmounted by a simple cornice. A plain margin surrounds the oblong ceiling, which is reduced to a square by a narrow panel at each end, filled with honeysuckle and foliated stems between husk festoons. Within the square a delicately reeded moulding forms a large circular panel which in turn encloses a strongly defined octagon, from the angles of which extend interlacing festoons of husks, the spaces thus formed being decorated with scrolls, branches and trophies. Within the octagon is a central seed, surrounded by radiating branches of honeysuckle and foliage, linked by festoons of leaves'.

That is the description of an expert — meticulously precise, but rather cold. To me, the ceiling was a fascinating web of fragile curlicues, skilfully framed in geometrical surrounds. It must have taken months to complete; and I often envisaged the plasterer, the pattern at his elbow, painstakingly creating those convoluted shapes and fixing them, with patient accuracy, on to the ceiling. In a small and very humble way, he must have known something of the dedication that sustained Michelangelo on his lofty platform in the Sistine Chapel.

That ceiling delighted me almost as much as the noble curve of the Crescent's façade, embellished with its stately array of Ionic columns — surely one of the outstanding townscapes of Europe. Ison describes it as being 'at once the finest building in Bath, and the greatest single achievement in the whole field of our urban architecture'. When I first lived there I wondered whether, seeing it day after day, my own euphoria would evaporate. In fact, it never diminished at all: whenever I rounded the corner of Brock Street, homeward bound, I always marvelled at its elegant beauty and magnificent proportions. Like any other great work of art, its appeal is timeless.

*View of Royal Crescent from the east, 18th century watercolour by Thomas Malton junior; No 1 Royal Crescent (below) is now the home of Bath Preservation Trust and is open to the public during the summer months.*

*From Thomas Rowlandson's* Comforts of Bath: *The Bath Races, with invalids frolicking before a stylised Royal Crescent; and in contrast (below) a fashionable music recital in progress.*

# II   Bath in the Eighteenth Century

The King's Circus and the Royal Crescent were the twin pinnacles of
Bath's eighteenth-century architectural development — a development that was prompted by the city's growing popularity as a spa.
Royalty had set the pattern at the outset, when Charles II came to
take the waters in 1663. Later, James II arrived, with his second wife,
Mary of Modena. Soon after their visit Mary became pregnant; she
eventually bore a son who was to become the father of the Young
Pretender, Bonnie Prince Charlie. In those days it was thought that
the waters encouraged fecundity, and a contemporary writer went
so far as to assert that, after one visit to Bath 'ladies often proved
with child even in their husbands' absence'. The reputation of the
thermal springs was becoming formidable indeed.

Queen Anne, we know, took the waters in the hope that they
would cure her gout; she suffered greatly in the knee and the foot
from this painful malady, and had to be carried to her coronation in
1702. But within a few years, other members of the royal family were
visiting Bath for social as well as medical reasons. Two of George
II's children — Prince Frederick and Princess Amelia — favoured
the city with their presence on more than one occasion, and
the nobility and the gentry were not slow to follow their
example.

The eldest of George II's eight children, Frederick Louis, Prince of
Wales, was an unremarkable character, of whom someone later
observed that 'there was no more to be said but that he was alive,
and is dead'. His father disliked him intensely, calling him 'a monster,
and the greatest villain that was ever born'. In 1737 he was ordered
to quit St James's Palace on account of his inconsiderate behaviour
at the lying-in of his wife. Yet in the following year, when he
visited Bath, the great Beau Nash honoured him by erecting the
obelisk which still stands in the centre of Queen Square. It was
designed by John Wood the elder, and cost £80; and Alexander
Pope, tongue in cheek no doubt, composed the banal inscription
that it carries. Frederick's reputation was well known, but as Prince
of Wales and heir to the throne, his presence was a decided asset, as
Nash well knew; and as Frederick presented him with a handsome

gold snuff-box before leaving, there must have been mutual grounds for satisfaction.

Frederick's sister, Princess Amelia, was another royal problem child: she was a raffish young woman who gambled excessively, swore like a trooper, and often dressed in eccentric fashion. She visited Bath seven times — which, again, was good for the city's reputation, however questionable was hers — and she usually stayed at what is now Amelia House, on South Parade. On her first visit, when she was a girl of seventeen, she was given an unexpected taste of the authority that Beau Nash exercised in the course of his public duty. He always insisted on ending dances in the Assembly Rooms at eleven o'clock precisely. One night, as he silenced the orchestra at the appointed time, Amelia called for an encore. 'One more dance, Mr Nash' she demanded imperiously, 'Remember, I am a Princess!' Nash's brandy-coloured face remained impassive. 'Yes, madam' he replied, 'but I reign here, and my laws must be kept'. The dance, and the argument, ended forthwith.

Bath was to enjoy more enlightened patronage than that provided by Frederick and Amelia. But the social pattern was by now firmly established, and the Bath road from London resounded to the rumble of wheels and thud of hooves, as more and more coaches trundled westwards, carrying a throng of assorted characters to the city. Aristocrats, squires, professional men, writers, philosophers, rakes, women — both austerely respectable and unashamedly vulgar — musicians, actors, dancing-masters, con-men — they all jolted to Bath in badly-sprung coaches, hell-bent on pleasure or profit, with a sizeable majority longing for both.

The building boom was thus inevitable; more and more lodging houses were urgently needed, and other facilities were proving sadly inadequate. A new theatre was built in Orchard Street in 1749, and two years later the old Pump Room was enlarged.* John Wood the elder transformed what became known as the Upper Town, creating Queen Square, Gay Street and the Circus; and his son, the younger Wood, not only added the Royal Crescent, but designed and completed the new Assembly Rooms immediately to the east of the Circus (1769–71).

---

*It was eventually demolished completely, and the present Pump Room was erected in 1792–95.

Bath was becoming a beautiful city; and as its fame spread, more and more notable people were inexorably drawn towards it. Politicians and statesmen realised that its ambience was relaxing: Burke and William Pitt, Earl of Chatham, visited it regularly, and Wilberforce knew it well. Artists like Gainsborough and Lawrence found it both salubrious and profitable. Poets, playwrights and novelists came — Wordsworth, Shelley, Oliver Goldsmith, Jane Austen, and later, Dickens and Walter Savage Landor. Heroes admired it, too — Clive, Nelson and Wolfe all stayed in the city. And, inevitably, the wits and the sages were unable to keep away. Dr Johnson followed Mrs Thrale to Bath, and stayed at the old Pelican Inn in Walcot Street; Lord Chesterfield was a regular visitor for thirty years; and even the delicately esoteric Horace Walpole, letter-writer supreme, stayed for three months — although he ultimately confessed to a profound dislike for the place.

Some of these well-known figures — notably Pitt, Clive and Gainsborough — had houses in the Circus. But few, surprisingly, chose to live in the Crescent. Horace Walpole would never have tolerated the walk up Gay Street: 'one cannot stir out of the town without clambering' he once wrote peevishly to a friend from his house in Chapel Court. Wordsworth, Goldsmith and Nelson preferred lodgings near the Parades; and Sam Johnson was far happier in the lively atmosphere of the 'Pelican' than he would ever have been in the drawing-room of a house in the Upper Town.

Nevertheless, the Crescent has had its share of interesting residents. Walk round the great curve from the Brock Street end, and inspect the bronze tablets that adorn the walls of some of the houses. There are five of them, if you include 1A, adjoining the return frontage of No 1, and they record the tenancies of Professor George Saintsbury, Christopher Anstey, the Linley family, Frederick Harrison and Sir Isaac Pitman. Not a remarkable muster of celebrated names, you may say, and with some justification. But there were others who never achieved the distinction of a bronze tablet, yet who were famous — even, in two or three cases, infamous — in their own time. And there was royalty, too, in the person of George III's second son, the Duke of York — the famous Duke of the nursery rhyme; he lived at No 1, and later at No 16, whenever he visited Bath. Altogether, the Crescent's well-known residents make up a richly varied cross-section of Engish life over a period of more than two hundred years.

Before looking at them in greater detail, it may be of interest to discuss the bronze tablets that appear on many of Bath's houses, identifying the residences and lodgings of famous people, and adding greatly to the enjoyment of a walk through the city streets. These were the idea of Thomas Sturge Cotterell, a former mayor and alderman of Bath, who was also a well-known local historian and, for several years, chairman of the Libraries Committee. As a result of his zealous efforts to publicise the city and its attractions, the Corporation approved a grant of £250 to erect 45 tablets. That was in 1898. The tablets were designed by Samuel Reay, a Bath architect, and their cost was rather less than £5 each — and that included the labour charges for fixing them in position on house walls.

It should be remembered that most of the celebrities who made the tiresome journey from London — it took almost two days by coach in the eighteenth century — rented houses for the season: very few of them owned property in Bath. Even Gainsborough, who lived and worked in the city for sixteen years, never owned his house in the Circus; he was a tenant of a Mr Penny, and paid a quarterly rate of thirteen shillings and fourpence (at a time when he was charging thirty guineas for a head, and eighty guineas for a full-length portrait). In these circumstances it was often very difficult to identify houses correctly, and mistakes in the siting of tablets was not unusual (it happened in Gainsborough's case). Nevertheless, Thomas Sturge Cotterell's brainwave has provided a source of pleasure and interest for countless twentieth-century visitors to Bath.

The first tablet was unveiled in 1898, and commemorated Sir William Herschel, musician and astronomer-extraordinary, who lived at 19 New King Street. He was musical director at the Assembly Rooms for several years, and won national fame in 1781 when, pursuing his hobby of astronomy, he discovered the planet Uranus; the following year he left Bath to take up the prestigious post of Astronomer Royal. It has been said that Keats' famous lines 'Then I felt like some watcher of the skies, When a new planet swims into his ken'* were inspired by Herschel's achievement.

---

*From the sonnet 'On first looking into Chapman's Homer'.

In 1902 the Earl of Rosebery, the famous Liberal statesman, came to Bath to unveil two more tablets in the city, commemorating the elder and younger Pitt. Lord Rosebery was chairman of the London County Council at that time, and he was so impressed with the bronze tablets that he expressed the hope that the County Council would adopt the same method. London's well-known blue and white circular plaques had been inaugurated in 1865 by the Royal Society of Arts. But as a result of Lord Rosebery's visit to Bath, the London County Council took over the task of publicly identifying famous houses, and in 1903 the first plaque under the Council's aegis was unveiled — by Lord Rosebery — at Holly Lodge, Campden Hill, the London home of Lord Macaulay. The houses of Disraeli, Dickens and Sir Robert Peel were similarly commemorated during the following months.

There are two or three bronze ornamental tablets, similar to those at Bath, to be seen in London; one adorns the house at 39 Montagu Square, Marylebone, where Anthony Trollope lived for some years. But in the main, London has remained faithful to the familiar blue and white plaques that were instituted more than a century ago.

# III  Number One The Crescent

The entrances to the first and last houses in the Royal Crescent —
Nos 1 and 30 — are on return frontages at each end of the great
curve. Neither bears a plaque commemorating a notable resident —
although there is one on the facade of 1A, commemorating the
tenancy of Professor George Saintsbury. But No 1 itself is an
interesting house in many respects. It is now owned by the Bath
Preservation Trust, and furnished and equipped in late eighteenth-
century style. During the summer months visitors can stroll through
its elegant rooms, and savour much of the atmosphere of Georgian
Bath.

The first leaseholder was Thomas Brock, brother-in-law of the
younger John Wood, and the man whose name was given to the
street connecting the Circus and the Crescent. Brock was a Cheshire
man, and was Town Clerk of Chester from 1756 until his death in
1785. He met the two Woods, father and son, in Liverpool, when the
elder Wood was designing the city's new town hall in 1749–50.
Two years later, the younger Wood married Brock's sister Elizabeth,
and Brock became his trustee. No doubt the Town Clerk of Chester
came down to Bath to appraise his brother-in-law's new Crescent,
and took the lease of No 1; but his duties in Chester could not have
allowed him much time to enjoy it. In 1778 a Mr Henry Sandford
was paying the rates; and in 1786 the house was advertised to let at
the inclusive rental of £140 per annum — a very high figure indeed
in those days, and one that proves how desirable lodgings in the
Crescent must have been.

In that same year — 1786 — an important visitor from France
lodged at No 1. She was Marie Thérèse Louise de Savoie Carignon,
Princesse de Lamballe, friend and lady-in-waiting to Queen Marie-
Antoinette. According to the *Bath Chronicle* of 27th September,
1786, she arrived with a large retinue of servants, and her personal
physician. She was a pale, slim lady with curly, fair hair, and a
prominent nose. She was abnormally sensitive; if she suffered the
slightest shock, she would collapse into a faint that often lasted for
two hours. The smell of violets made her disastrously ill, and the
sight of shellfish, even in a painting, sent her into a nervous fit. She

seems to have had more allergies than personal names and titles, and it's easy to understand why her physician always travelled with her. But Marie-Antoinette adored her.

We don't know how long she stayed in Bath on tnat occasion. She returned to England in 1791, when the French Revolution was at its height, hoping to persuade the British royal family to help Louis XVI and Marie-Antoinette to escape from France. As the terror grew, and the slaughter of aristocrats increased, Antoinette urged her to remain in England and ensure her own safety. But she went back to Paris; and in 1792 she died horribly, as the Revolution reached its bloody climax in the September Massacres. She was dragged from a prison cell by the mob, robbed of her belongings, killed, and her severed head was paraded through the streets on a spike. Among her few possessions on that fearful day was a ring containing a lock of Marie-Antoinette's hair, with the inscription 'Misfortune has turned it white'.

But the most celebrated of No 1's residents was undoubtedly George III's second son, Frederick Augustus, Duke of York. He took the house for a period in 1796; on 7th April that year, the *Chronicle* announced that 'the Duke of York has engaged the first house in the Crescent, late Mr Sandford's, as his residence'. On several subsequent visits he lodged at No 16, now part of the Royal Crescent Hotel.

The Duke was no stranger to Bath; he visited the spa in 1795 with his wife, attended the opening of the new Pump Room, and was presented with the freedom of the city. No doubt he enjoyed the occasion immensely. He had just returned from an arduous military campaign in Flanders, where he had commanded the English army — not with conspicuous success — in the war against revolutionary France: he had been ordered home, and consoled with a Field-Marshal's baton. So Bath must have seemed relaxing. We know he enjoyed taking the waters, because a month or so after his visit in April, 1796, the *Chronicle* reported that 'a return of spasmodic affections of the stomach, of which the Duke of York was happily relieved in the winter by the Bath water, has determined his Royal Highness to revisit this city as soon as his absence from London can be dispensed with. Some of the domesticks are arrived at His Highness's house in the Crescent'.

The Duke was thirty-three years old at this time, and his reputation was little better than that of his elder brother the Prince of Wales, who later became the Prince Regent; he was self-indulgent to a degree, and his capacity for wine and women, as well as his passion for gambling, was legendary. Later, when he became commander-in-chief of the army, he tempered his wayward habits a good deal, and indeed did much to improve the army's standards and efficiency. But in 1809 he was involved in a most unsavoury scandal. His mistress, an actress known as Mrs Mary Anne Clarke, was accused of taking bribes to procure — through the Duke — promotions for senior army officers. After weeks of public enquiry and widespread gossip he was exonerated from blame, but was relieved of his command; and although he was reinstated two years later, his reputation was damaged beyond repair. Perhaps it's appropriate that he is chiefly remembered, for most of us, as the hero of a nursery rhyme, marching ten thousand men to the top of a hill, and then marching them down again.

The Duke of York's tenancy of No 1 ended in 1796, and for the next two or three years the house was leased to a Mr Henry Milsom. This gentleman was a lodging-house keeper, and he had no connection with Milsom Street; the developer of that prestigious thoroughfare was Daniel Milsom, a wine cooper. During the nineteenth century No 1, more often than not, was a lodging-house. A Colonel Doveton, whose father had known Napoleon on St Helena, lived there for some time; and an Irish cleric rejoicing in the name and title of the Honourable and Reverend James St Leger, Rector of Castletown Roche, County Cork, held the lease for three years. From 1840 to 1846, the house was a seminary for young ladies, presided over, no doubt with stern Victorian propriety, by a Miss Eliza Evans. The last private resident was Mr Pryce Norman, owner of a jewellery business in Bristol: he lived there from 1959 to 1967.

In 1967 the fate of No 1 changed dramatically. Major Bernard Cayzer, a member of a well-known shipping family, saw the house advertised in 'Country Life', and promptly bought it. Then he presented it to the Bath Preservation Trust, together with a handsome sum to help in its restoration and redecoration. Spurred on, no doubt, by this very generous act of philanthropy, the Historic Buildings Council and the Pilgrim Trust also made generous contributions and the famous old house was thus restored to its pristine glory. Other benefactors gave or lent items of furniture and pictures, and in June, 1970, No 1 was opened to the public as an eighteenth-century domestic museum.

The attention to detail was commendably exact. On the ground floor the library, with its splendid portrait of George III, and its Chippendale mahogany bureau bookcase, is the type of room in which Henry Milsom might have worked. The dining room is equipped in a manner that would surely have pleased Thomas Brock; and the drawing room, with its portrait of the Duchess of Devonshire, and its Chippendale card table and Hepplewhite chairs, would have evoked a grunt of approval from the Duke of York. The bedroom, needless to say, with a Louis XVI bed, and kidney-shaped table with ormolu mounts, would have made the Princesse de Lamballe swoon with homesickness.

Period detail was faithfully observed on the exterior of the building, too. At various times during the nineteenth century, owners of houses in the Crescent had the sills of their first-floor windows lowered, and the original glazing bars removed, in order to instal the new, much larger panes that the Bristol glassmakers were eager to supply. The Crescent's No 1, you will notice, has the original, shorter windows on the first floor, and the glazing bars have been restored at all levels.

# IV    Christopher Anstey

The bronze tablet on the wall of No 5 Royal Crescent is considered by some researchers into the arcane history of Bath to be wrongly sited — and, indeed, to be wrongly inscribed. It commemorates the tenancy of Christopher Anstey, from 1770 until 1805. But the Bath rate books show that Anstey lived at No 4; a Mr Bathoe was the tenant of No 5, although Anstey, for some reason, paid the rates of No 5 until 1789. In 1792 he moved to the recently completed Marlborough Buildings nearby: he was fifty-eight years old then, and perhaps welcomed the opportunity to take a smaller house.

Anstey's claim to fame and a bronze tablet rests solely on a slim book called *The New Bath Guide*. It was published in 1766, and it became an immediate bestseller, running through ten editions in the decade following its publication, and creating a mild sensation in half the drawing rooms of London and Bath. It is still available, and still worth reading — an inspired little cameo, perceptive, witty, vulgar in parts, and greatly entertaining.

It isn't a guide in the accepted sense of the word; it is a satirical review, in verse, of fashionable society in Bath in the mid-eighteenth century. It describes, in the form of letters to their family, the experiences of a young man, Simkin Blunderhead, and his cousin Jenny, when they spend a season in the city, taking the waters and enjoying the many diversions that Bath then had to offer. The metre is chiefly anapaestic — four beats to the line — and the rhythm is smooth and pleasing. Barham used the same type of metre in his *Ingoldsby Legends*, and W. S. Gilbert's *Bab Ballads* owe much to it, too. Here is Simkin writing to his mother, soon after his arrival in Bath:

> 'The Captain's a worthy good sort of a man,
> For he calls in upon us whenever he can,
> And often a dinner or supper he takes here,
> And Jenny and he talk of Milton and Shakespeare,
> For the life of me now, I can't think of his name,
> But we all got acquainted as soon as we came'.

The Captain, of course, was one of those smooth characters who

26

profited handsomely from the gullibility of pleasure-seeking visitors:
he had his eye not only on Simkin's purse, but on Jenny's virtue, as
subsequent events showed. Meanwhile, Simkin was keeping his
mother abreast of the news, and suggesting that the whole family
should live in Bath:

> 'Our neighbour, Sir Easterlin Widgeon, has swore
> He'll never return to his bogs any more;
> The Thickskulls are settled; we've had invitations
> With a great many more on the score of relations;
> The Loungers are come too: old Stucco has just sent
> His plan for a house to be built in the Crescent;
> 'Twill soon be complete, and they say all their work
> Is as strong as St Paul's, or the minster at York.
> Don't you think 'twould be better to lease our estate,
> And buy a good house here before 'tis too late?
> You never can go, my dear mother, where you
> So much have to see, and so little to do.'

Some of the anatomical details included in Simkin's letters earned
Anstey considerable censure: there was a good deal of coarseness
in eighteenth-century life, but not everyone approved of it appearing
in print. Here's the young hopeful once more, writing home about
his current complaints:

> 'But the noise I have heard in my bowels like thunder,
> Is a flatus, I find, in my left hypochonder . . .
> Five times have I purged, yet I'm sorry to tell ye,
> I find the same gnawing and wind in my belly'.

Nobody, of course, claimed that the poem was anything other than
a clever and amusing satire: to *literati* weaned on the splendid
apostrophes of Dryden and Pope, it was certainly not good poetry.
But it struck a remarkably responsive chord in the imagination of a
wider public. Even Horace Walpole, than whom there were few
sterner critics, was delighted with it. 'There is a new thing published' he wrote to his friend George Montagu, 'that will make you
bepiss your cheeks with laughter . . . describing the life of Bath,
and incidentally everything else — but so much wit, so much
humour, fun, poetry, so much originality, never met together

before . . . I can say it by heart, though a quarto, and if I had time would write it down, for it is not yet reprinted, and not one to be had'.

As we have seen, no less than ten editions of the book appeared in the ten years following its publication. After the second edition was published, Anstey sold the copyright to his publisher, James Dodsley, for two hundred and fifty pounds. Dodsley, delighted with the book's success, returned the copyright to the author as a gift when the tenth edition appeared, confessing that the profits from the book were greater than from any other title he had published during the same period.

Anstey's receipt for the reimbursement was at one time to be seen in the Mayor's Room in Bath's Guildhall. It reads: 'July 31, 1766. Received of Mr Dodsley, the sum of two hundred and fifty pounds in full for the sole right of the copy of the New Bath Guide. Witness my hand, Chr. Anstey'. The proceeds of the transaction were donated to the Mineral Water Hospital.

Anstey was born in 1724 at Brinkley in Cambridgeshire, and was educated at Eton and King's College, Cambridge. He became a Fellow of King's in 1745, and a year later took his degree. Then he ran into trouble with the college authorities. They had introduced an innovation into degree ceremonies that required graduates to compose, and speak, a long declamation in Latin. Anstey produced an absurdly verbose speech — 'a rhapsody of adverbs' as one of his sons was later to describe it — pouring censure and ridicule on the whole proceeding. His degree was annulled; and twenty years later, in *The New Bath Guide*, he recalled the occasion:

> 'At Granta, sweet Granta where, studious of ease
> Seven years did I sleep, and then lost my degrees',

He remained a Fellow of King's for seven or eight years and then, when he was 32, he married the daughter of a wealthy Hertfordshire brewer, and settled down to manage the estate his father had bequeathed him. After an attack of 'bilious fever', he visited Bath and took the waters; and on returning to Cambridgeshire, he sat down and wrote *The New Bath Guide*. The book's success no doubt encouraged him to reject the role of country squire; in 1770 he moved permanently to Bath, and took one of the newly-completed

28

houses in the Royal Crescent. His marriage was a successful one, and he and his wife lived contentedly together for nearly half a century; he described her as 'the pattern of virtue, and the source of all my happiness'. There were thirteen children of the marriage, but only eight survived their father.

A portrait of Anstey hangs in the magnificent Banqueting Room in the Guildhall at Bath. It was painted by William Hoare, and it shows a dark-haired, good-looking man in early middle age; he wears a sage-green coat, braided with gold, and a long white waistcoat, unbuttoned at the top, into which his left hand is thrust, in the Napoleonic manner. His unlined, fresh-complexioned face has an undeniable air of tranquillity and contentment. He looks every inch a successful and happy man — a best-selling author, savouring the acclaim his work had brought him.

Yet oddly enough, Anstey wrote nothing else of any consequence. In *The Cambridge History of English Literature*, Professor Saintsbury refers to *The New Bath Guide*, and adds that 'he never wrote any other that was of even the slightest value'. Much, indeed, of his later work was trivial. Three years after coming to Bath, he produced a short poem with the promising title *Ode to an Evening View of the Crescent, 1773*. It is a justified criticism of Sir Peter Rivers Gay, who had put forward a scheme to convert 'the beautiful fields of the Crescent at Bath' into vegetable gardens. But the verse itself is sheer doggerel. There are twenty-five short stanzas, each one ending with the words 'Sir Peter Rivers Gay'. Here are two examples:

'Now on yon Crescent's form so fair
My ravished eyes shall stay,
View all Palladio's beauties there,
Sir Peter Rivers Gay.

For Oh! I tremble to relate
Thine ills in future days —
A Collyflow'r must be thy fate,
Sir Peter Rivers Gay.'

Clearly the Muse had deserted him. A later poem, *The Election Ball*, won some modest acclaim from the critics, but he was never

able to achieve anything that remotely approached the success of
*The New Bath Guide.*

He had occasion to take Sir Peter Rivers Gay to task again a few
years later. Before 1790 the land behind the Royal Crescent, on
which St James's Square now stands, was cultivated by residents of
the Crescent — compensating them, to some extent, for the absence
of gardens attached to the houses. Anstey enjoyed working on his
plot; and he was deeply annoyed when, in March 1790, Sir Peter,
who owned the land, granted building leases to two developers.
Not surprisingly, Anstey protested in verse, and the quatrain he
wrote was widely quoted:

> 'Ye men of Bath, who stately mansions rear
> To await for tenants from the De'il knows where,
> Would you pursue a plan that cannot fail?
> Erect a madhouse, and enlarge your jail'.

Outbursts such as this, however, were rare, and his equanimity
seems seldom to have been disturbed. His second son, John, edited a
complete edition of his poems in 1808, and in an introduction he
described his father's long life as being 'unimpeded by sickness and
unclouded by sorrow, or any serious misfortune: his life was a life
of temperance, of self-denial, and of moderation in all things'.

Filial piety can make a paragon of a man: yet not all of Anstey's
contemporaries found him exemplary. Fanny Burney was singu-
larly unimpressed when, with Mrs Thrale, she met him in May,
1780, at a social gathering in Bath. She may have been irritated by
the recollection that, two years previously, when the authorship of
her novel *Evelina* was undisclosed, there had been many who believed
that Anstey had written it. Meeting him face to face, she found him
dull and a trifle pompous. In her diary she noted: 'Afterwards, who
should be announced but the author of *The Bath Guide*, Mr Anstey;
I was now all eye; but not being able to be all ear, I heard but little
that he said, and that little was scarcely worth hearing. He had no
opportunity of shining, and was as much like another man as you
can imagine'. After another meeting, later that same May, she wrote:
'Mr Anstey opens rather more, and approaches nearer to being
agreeable. If he could but forget he had written the *New Bath Guide*,
with how much more pleasure would everybody else remember it'.

Mrs Montagu, the celebrated blue-stocking, who lived for a time at No 16 the Crescent, was more charitable: in a letter written from Bath in 1779, she confided to a friend: 'Mr Anstey was often with me, and you will believe he is very droll and entertaining; but what recommends him more, is his great attention to his family. He has eight children. He instructs his boys in Greek and Latin, so that they are fitted for the upper forms of Eton School, where their education is finished. He has a house in the Crescent, at which he resides the greatest part of the year. Mrs Anstey is a very sensible, amiable woman, and does not deal in the gossip of the place'.

All in all, Anstey appears to have been a gentle, scholarly man, devoted to his family and, Miss Burney notwithstanding, far from boastful. He enjoyed the company of his friends, and loved to entertain them at his hospitable table; and his regular habits, together with a distaste for excess, prolonged his good health considerably. But the years inevitably took their toll. Early in 1805 he became seriously ill for probably the first time in his life, and was taken to his son-in-law's house near Chippenham in Wiltshire; and there, in his 81st year, he died, 'without any apparent pain, in the midst of his surrounding family, and in possession of his admirable faculties to the last.' He was buried in Bath, at Walcot Church.

In the epilogue to the second edition of *The New Bath Guide* Anstey wrote:

'Give bustos to poets of higher reknown,
I ne'er was ambitious in marble to frown'

— lines that might be said to demonstrate an awareness of his limitations as a poet. He was, however, too modest; after his death, a memorial tablet was dedicated to him, and placed in Poets' Corner in Westminster Abbey, where it can still be seen. He will always be remembered as the man whose nimble verse satirised the foibles of eighteenth-century Bath.

# V Elizabeth Linley and Sheridan

Anstey lived in the Crescent for twenty-two years, from 1770 to 1792. They were important and eventful years in many ways. The American colonists issued their Declaration of Independence in 1776, and finally achieved that independence in 1783. The French Revolution erupted in 1789, and was later to involve much of Europe in a protracted war. And in England itself the Industrial Revolution, motivated by new inventions like the steam engine and the spinning jenny, was slowly but surely establishing itself. It was to change the whole fabric of British society within a few decades.

Anstey's life, however, was unaffected by these momentous events. As a country squire residing comfortably in Bath, he was fairly typical of English upper middle class society in the second half of the eighteenth century. His exemplary self-discipline was perhaps a little unusual at that time; but he belonged to a comparatively widespread social coterie, with the aristocracy at its head, wealthy enough to indulge their individual tastes and eccentricities at leisure. Many were well educated, chiefly in the classics, and helped to establish standards of taste and artistic discrimination that still excite our admiration today. Others were reckless ne'er-do-wells, squandering their wealth in the pursuit of pleasure, yet always retaining pride in what they called their 'bottom' — a word that was regularly used to describe pluck or spirit. Collectively, they gave to the century a character, an individuality that has distinguished it to this day.

English society at that time was uniquely stable. It was an age of well-defined social distinctions, characterised by a degree of self-complacency that did much to inhibit movements towards reform. G. M. Trevelyan has aptly described it as a society 'with a mental outlook of its own, self-poised, self-judged, and self-approved, freed from the disturbing passions of the past, and not yet troubled with anxieties about a very different future which was soon to be brought upon the scene by the Industrial and the French Revolutions. The gods mercifully gave mankind this little moment of peace between the religious fanaticisms of the past, and the fanaticisms of class and race that were speedily to arise and dominate time to come'.

In this halcyon climate the patricians flourished inordinately. To

*A Modern Belle* *going to the* *Rooms* *at* *Bath.*

Pub.<sup></sup> Jan.<sup>y</sup> 13.<sup>th</sup> 1796. by
H. Humphrey, New Bond Street.

The Royal Crescent Hotel — 1. the magnificent 18th century stucco ceiling in the Duke of York Suite; 2. the Sir Percy Blakeney Suite with 17th century four poster; 3. entrance hall, with portrait by Reynolds.

quote Trevelyan again: 'Perhaps no set of men and women since the world began, enjoyed so many different sides of life, with so much zest, as the English upper class at this period'. Their counterparts in France were shortly to experience the horrors of the tumbril and the guillotine: but the English nobility and gentry remained firmly at the top of the social pyramid, secure, self-assured, often idiosyncratic. They gambled heavily and continuously, and almost any topic under the sun was worth a wager. One day a man collapsed outside a London club, and the inmates immediately began to bet on whether or not he was alive: they even objected to someone giving the poor fellow resuscitation, in case it affected the outcome of the bet. In 1770 Walpole wrote: 'The gaming is worthy the decline of an Empire. The young men lose five, ten, fifteen thousand pounds in an evening. Lord Stavordale, not one-and-twenty, lost eleven thousand last Tuesday, but recovered it by one great hand at hazard'. Recklessness was matched by imperturbability; when they lost heavily at cards, they tried to show their unconcern by falling asleep at the table or, like Charles James Fox, retiring to a corner to read Herodotus. Their casual attitude to money was typified by Lord Durham, who earned himself the sobriquet of 'King Jog' when he remarked that one could 'jog along on £40,000 a year'. And that, remember, was about two hundred years ago.

They were not all gamblers and irresponsible spendthrifts, by any means. A great many of them actively encouraged the arts, and a high degree of literacy was a quality they admired and respected; it was for this reason that they welcomed the company of Dr Johnson, in spite of his nondescript dress and his avowed unconcern for the social graces. Lord Chesterfield underlined the importance that was attached to correct expression and spelling, when he wrote to his son in 1750: 'I must tell you that orthography, in the true sense of the word, is so absolutely necessary for a man of letters, or a gentleman, that one false spelling may fix a ridicule upon him for the rest of his life: and I know a man of quality who never recovered the ridicule of having spelled "wholesome" without the "w"'.

These, then, were the people who helped to mould the character of English society in the second half of the eighteenth century. Their life styles embodied extremes of wisdom and foolishness, philanthropy and profligacy, tenderness and cruelty, brilliance and dullness. They loved pleasure — another of their favourite words was 'agrémens' — and they believed they were the salt of the earth. A great many of them came to Bath at one time or another, taking houses for a season or a few weeks, and bringing in their train a small army of less fortunate souls who hoped to profit from their extravagances. In one year, no less than four dukes, twenty-four earls, fourteen viscounts and twelve barons figured in the list of visitors. Prominent writers, artists, actors and politicians were frequently to be seen in the coffee houses and on the Parades. It was the high noon of Bath's fame as a fashionable resort.

Anstey lived in the city at the very height of this dazzling period. He took his house in the Royal Crescent in 1770; and during the next few years he witnessed the comings and goings of an impressive number of well-known people, all of them seeking pleasure, relaxation or profit in Bath's agreeable surroundings. Some, like Gainsborough and Sarah Siddons, came to work; others, like Nelson, to convalesce. Dr Johnson came in pursuit of Mrs Thrale; but he was well aware of the city's benevolent qualities, as he proved when he replied to a lady who had written to him to tell him how unhappy she was: 'Let me counsel you not to waste your health in unprofitable sorrow, but go to Bath and endeavour to prolong your life'. A large majority endorsed this view completely and came, like Lord Chesterfield, to assuage the agonies of their gout, or to dispel the vapours, and to have a thoroughly enjoyable time in the process. And the gamblers and the soldiers of fortune came too, to prey on the susceptible and the unwary; Anstey, as we shall see, had one or two prime examples of these gentry as his close neighbours in the Crescent.

The great Master of the Ceremonies, Beau Nash, had died in 1761. But the code of conduct that he had imposed during his long reign still remained, and decorum and a degree of formality still characterised most of the public entertainments. Nash's rule that gentlemen should not wear swords was strictly observed. Gambling, of course, was still widely practised, although a law of 1745 had curtailed its excessiveness in public places. The theatre was excitingly alive, with Henderson and Mrs Siddons appearing regularly before enthusiastic audiences; there were concerts and balls in the new Upper Assembly Rooms, completed in 1771; and the Pump Room and the Parades were thronged with elegantly dressed pleasure-seekers who gossiped their powdered heads off from mid-morning until late afternoon.

The chatter was usually inconsequential enough: perhaps an acid comment on some titled lady's gown at the last cotillion ball, or a reproving word or two about some sprig of a noble family who had squandered his patrimony at hazard or faro. But in the spring of 1772 there was a succulent piece of local scandal that made patrician tongues wag faster than ever. Elizabeth Linley, a beautiful girl of eighteen, already famous as an accomplished singer, and living respectably with her family in the Royal Crescent, had eloped to France with an Irish dreamer who cherished ambitions to become a playwright. His name was Richard Brinsley Sheridan.

Anstey, I imagine, was not a man who approved of gossip; but he must have heard about this local sensation at an early stage, because the Linley family were his neighbours — their house in the Crescent was No 11 (there is now a bronze tablet on the wall, recording their tenancy and Elizabeth's elopement). And Mrs Anstey, one feels, would have been less than human had she not discussed the matter with her husband at some length. It was a major topic of conversation in the city for weeks.

The Linleys were a remarkable family. Thomas Linley was a musical entrepreneur who arranged concerts in Bath, gave singing lessons, and played the harpsichord expertly. His two elder daughters, Elizabeth and Mary, were singers of considerable ability; and his son Thomas was a highly talented violinist who visited Italy as a child prodigy in 1770, won the friendship and approbation of Mozart, and died tragically in a boating accident at the age of twenty-two.

The family had lived in Bath for many years. Their first house was in Abbey Green. In 1764 they moved to Pierrepoint Place, close to the Doric archway that links Orchard Street and Pierrepoint Street. Finally, with Elizabeth and Mary firmly established as concert singers, they took a house in Royal Crescent in the autumn of 1771. The two sisters performed frequently at the new Upper Assembly Rooms nearby, and Thomas Linley arranged many concerts here; the move was a convenient one, and reflected their increasing prosperity.

Elizabeth was undoubtedly the brightest star in this gifted constellation. She was beautiful: this is abundantly evident from her portraits, painted by Gainsborough and Reynolds. And there were a great many impartial auditors who testified to the fact that she sang divinely. One of these was William Jackson, organist at Exeter Cathedral, who wrote: 'Her voice was remarkably sweet, and her scale just and perfect; from the lowest to the highest note the tone was of the same quality . . . Her genius and sense gave a consequence to her performance which no fool with the voice of an angel could ever attain'.

Reynolds painted her as St Cecilia, and the portrait was exhibited at the Royal Academy, where it created a mild sensation. The artist's nephew met her, and was entranced. 'I cannot suppose there was ever a greater beauty in the world' he enthused, 'Not even Helen or Cleopatra could have exceeded her'. At a Royal command performance at Drury Lane, George III gazed at her with much more than paternal interest. Among the audience was the ubiquitous Horace Walpole, and he couldn't resist a sly dig at the royal enthusiasm. 'Miss Linley's beauty is in the superlative degree' he told a friend, 'The King admires her, and ogles her as much as he dares to do in so holy a place as an oratorio'. And even that old reprobate John Wilkes fell under her spell. In January 1772 he noted in his diary: 'Breakfasted with Mr and the two Misses Linley . . . at Mr Linley's house in the Crescent'. Soon afterwards, in a letter to his daughter, he described the Linley girls: 'The eldest I think still superior to all the handsome things I have heard of her' he wrote, 'She does not seem in the least spoiled by the idle talk of our sex, and is the most modest, pleasing, delectable flower I have seen for a great while; the youngest a mere coquet; no sentiment. . . .'

It was hardly surprising that such a beautiful and talented girl should attract a host of male admirers. Among her most ardent suitors were a married man, Captain Thomas Mathews, two brothers, Charles and Richard Sheridan, an elderly gentleman, Walter Long, whose chief qualification was his wealth, and a passionate undergraduate from Oxford called Nathaniel Halhed. Halhed was a close friend of Richard Sheridan's, and after hearing Elizabeth sing in oratorio at Oxford, he wrote to him at Bath: 'I have just been to hear Miss Linley rehearse. I am petrified; my very faculties are annihilated with wonder. My conception could not form such a power of voice — such a melody — such a soft, yet so audible a tone . . .'. Even Sheridan, himself no mean exponent of the honeyed phrase, must have raised an eyebrow at such fulsome adulation.

Thomas Linley, shrewd business man that he was, regarded the young Elizabeth as a valuable financial asset, and he was concerned that she should marry suitably and well; under pressure from him, she became engaged to Mr Long late in 1770. But the betrothal, clearly an unsatisfactory one, lasted only a few months; in the summer of the following year Mr Long withdrew his claim to the lady, and compensated her handsomely with a cash gift of £3000, and jewels worth £1000.

Despite these undoubtedly generous parting gifts from her ageing lover, Elizabeth was depressed. She was upset by the publicity her engagement had received, and by the gossip occasioned by a new play, *The Maid of Bath* by Samuel Foote, whose plot was clearly based on her own emotional problems: she was dispirited, far from well, and contemplated running away to France. It was at this critical juncture that the enterprising Richard Brinsley Sheridan showed his hand.

His father, Thomas Sheridan, was an Irish actor who came to Bath in 1770 to teach elocution. Richard had recently left Harrow, after an undistinguished scholastic career, and yearned to write. He had admired the captivating Miss Linley for some time, but not as ardently as his elder brother, Charles. Now he decided to act. He supported Elizabeth's plans to leave her family, and he undertook to accompany her. On the evening of Wednesday, 18th March, 1772, when Thomas Linley and Mary were attending a concert, the couple left No 11 Royal Crescent, climbed into a waiting post-chaise — in which Sheridan had considerately installed a chaperone — and made their way to London. A day or so later they disembarked at Dunkirk. She was eighteen, he was twenty-one.

Sheridan, it seems, used the travelling time well. Months later, Elizabeth wrote to him describing her feelings on the journey. 'When I left Bath' she admitted, 'I had not an idea of you but as a friend. It was not your person that gained my affection. No, Sheridan, it was that delicacy, that tender passion, that interest which you seemed to take in my welfare, that were the motives that induced me to love you'.

The Royal Crescent

The couple were married in Calais by a priest 'accustomed to such unions'. They agreed to keep the marriage secret, and travelled on to Lille, where Elizabeth was admitted to the guest-house of a convent. She remained there until her father, having received a letter disclosing her whereabouts, arrived to take her back home. Mr Linley could easily have been misled by a report in one of the London papers, which was explicit but mistaken: 'Bath. Wednesday evening the eldest Miss Linley of this city, celebrated and admired for her musical abilities, set off with Mr Sheridan Jun. on a matrimonial expedition to Scotland'. He was, however, correctly apprised on time, and instead of dashing off to Gretna Green he sailed for France, and eventually accompanied both the lovers back to Bath.

Meanwhile Captain Mathews, another of Elizabeth's ardent admirers, was simmering with hostility towards Sheridan. He had paid Miss Linley a great deal of attention before the elopement, and she seems not to have discouraged him by any means. Now, incensed at the turn events had taken, he published a strongly-worded indictment of Sheridan's behaviour in the *Bath Chronicle*, and took himself off to London. After reading the accusing paragraph, Sheridan could scarcely restrain his own anger; he followed Mathews to London at once, and demanded satisfaction.

The two men fought with swords in an upstairs room of the Castle Tavern in Henrietta Street. Mathews was quickly disarmed, apparently by the sheer energy of Sheridan's initial assault. He begged for his life, and proffered an apology; and this, too, was eventually published in the *Bath Chronicle*. Honour had been appeased, and the acrimonious affair appeared to be over.

Mathews, however, was far from satisfied. More bitter words were exchanged, and this time it was the captain who issued a challenge. A second duel was fought at Kingsdown, near Bath, and it appears to have been a clumsy, ill-managed affair; the swords of both men were broken early in the fight, and at one stage they were wrestling on the ground and hacking desperately at each other with what remained of their blades. Both were wounded, but Mathews was on his feet quickly. 'I've done for him' he said to his seconds, looking down at Sheridan, whose clothes were stained with blood. Then he climbed into his carriage and was driven away. Later he was to suggest that Sheridan had arrived drunk at the scene of the duel, and

38

that the stains on his shirt were caused, not by blood, but by claret that he had vomited during the fight.

Sheridan was, however, badly hurt. He was taken to the White Hart Inn where his wounds were dressed by surgeons; and several weeks passed before he finally recovered.

After so much travail, he could surely have been forgiven for believing that he had earned the right to declare his love for Elizabeth openly, and to claim her as his wife. But Mr Linley and Sheridan's father were both strongly opposed to the union: the lovers were able to meet only clandestinely, and to exchange furtive letters and verses which were left for each other in a grotto on the banks of the Avon.

So far the story appears to have followed the classic plot line of a romantic novel. And, true to type, there was a happy sequel. Sheridan was sent to Waltham Abbey in Essex by his father; and Elizabeth, after being exiled to Wells for a period, resumed her professional engagements. She sang several times at Covent Garden, and they were able to meet. Gradually Mr Linley's opposition to the match evaporated; and on 13th April, 1773, they were married in London. The *Morning Chronicle* reported: 'Tuesday was married at Maryle-bone Church by the Rev Dr Booth, the celebrated Miss Linley to Mr Sheridan. After the ceremony they set out with her family and friends, and dined at the "Star and Garter" on Richmond Hill; and in the evening they had a ball after which the family and friends returned to town, and left the young couple at a gentleman's house at Mitcham to consummate their nuptials'.

For a time, all was more than well. Sheridan refused to allow Elizabeth to continue her career as a professional singer, but what now appears to us to be male chauvinism was the accepted order of things then; she still sang, but only at private concerts. Sheridan became proprietor of the theatre at Drury Lane. His first play, *The Rivals*, was produced in 1775, and his great masterpiece, *The School for Scandal*, two years later. In 1780 he was elected MP for Stafford, and achieved considerable fame as a politician, particularly with his speeches supporting the impeachment of Warren Hastings.

Bath saw the couple infrequently, so busy were their lives in London; Mr Linley became a partner of Sheridan's at Drury Lane, and the house in Royal Crescent was sold. But as the years passed, the marriage that had been achieved at so much cost became stormy, and the fault, it seems, lay with Sheridan's infidelity. As his political reputation grew, Elizabeth's health declined steadily. She developed tuberculosis, and died in 1792 at the age of thirty-eight. The scenario had changed dramatically: the theme of the romantic playlet had been transformed into the realm of grand opera.

# VI The Vicomte Du Barré and Philip Thicknesse

Sheridan's classic comedy *The School for Scandal*, was first produced in 1777. A year later, in October 1778, it was played for the first time in Bath, with Sarah Siddons in the role of Mrs Candour; the great actress was making her début before Bath audiences in that year, and she played the role eleven times during the season — for the princely salary of £3 per week.*

The season, like many at that period, was outstandingly successful; enthusiastic audiences filled the theatre for every performance, the balls and concerts in the Assembly Rooms were amply attended, and the coffee houses buzzed with the inconsequential gossip of a host of well-dressed idlers. That autumn of 1778, along with others in the same decade, witnessed the very pinnacle of Bath's fame as a pleasure resort. But for one visitor it brought sudden and violent death at the hand of a friend and close confederate.

He was a French nobleman, and his epitaph can still be seen on a tombstone in the churchyard at Bathampton, just outside Bath. It reads: 'Here rest the remains of Jean Baptiste du Barré. Obiit 18th November, 1778'. The brief statement is a sad little postscript to a heated quarrel that took place at No 8 Royal Crescent, and ended tragically on Claverton Down, in the cold light of a November dawn. No bronze tablet commemorates either the occasion, or the man who died: he was a professional gambler who had come to Bath with the sole intention of lightening the pockets and purses of those innumerable optimists who fancied their chances at a game of faro or hazard. Yet he was as typical of the Bath scene at that time as either Christopher Anstey or the Linley family.

Jean Baptiste, Vicomte du Barré, was said to be a relative of Madame du Barry, the famous courtesan and mistress of Louis XV. He arrived in Bath in the early autumn of 1778, accompanied by his wife and sister, and an Irish Jacobite, a Captain Rice, whose grand-

---

*Mrs Siddons was later invited to join the Drury Lane company in London, and she appeared there for the first time on October 10th, 1780, at a salary of £10 per week. She was an immediate success in a play called *The Fatal Marriage*; according to a contemporary, 'men wept, and women fainted or were carried out in fits of hysterics.' After four years, her salary had risen to 23 guineas per week.

father had served in the French army. A lease was taken on No 8 Royal Crescent, and lavish parties were given there. Both men were inveterate and skilful gamblers, and the two ladies were perfect hostesses. The parties were lively, successful affairs, and when the cards and dice were produced, the stakes were often recklessly high. The two gentlemen from France soon found themselves profiting handsomely.

Late one night they quarrelled over the sharing of £650 that they had won from a Colonel Champion. The guests had all left, and the brandy decanters were almost empty. The quarrel became increasingly bitter. Tempers were roused, accusations were made. Rice threw down his glove, and the challenge was immediately accepted by the Vicomte; a question of honour, even between friends, left him with no alternative. Accompanied by hastily appointed seconds, the two gamblers made their way to the Three Tuns Inn in Stall Street. Here an ostler was roused, a coach hired, and the party went on to Claverton Down. As a grey November dawn was breaking the ground was measured and staked, and pistols were primed. Du Barré fired first, and wounded his friend in the thigh. Rice's aim was more deadly: the Vicomte was hit in the chest, and died a few moments later. Rice was subsequently tried for manslaughter at Taunton, but was acquitted, and eventually went to Spain. Honour had been satisfied, 'bottom' had been proved and, at the end of it all, a man was dead. It is sobering to reflect that, if Sheridan had been obliged to use pistols in either of his duels with Captain Mathews — a military man who was familiar with firearms — the probability is that *The Rivals* and *The School for Scandal* would never have been written.

There was an interesting sequel to the Vicomte's death. The duel was fought on a Wednesday, and on the following Saturday evening Henderson appeared as Falstaff in the first part of Shakespeare's *King Henry IV* at the Bath Theatre. When he came to the lines 'What is honour? A word. What is that word honour? What is that honour? Air. A trim reckoning! Who hath it?' the actor paused deliberately, and went on 'He that died on Wednesday!' Needless to say, the words created a sensation in the packed house. There were many in the audience who thought that the last phrase was an impromptu addition. They were wrong; Henderson kept strictly to the text of the play. It was his sense of timing that made the passage so dramatically effective.

*   *   *

There is, as we have seen, no bronze tablet on the wall of No 8 the Crescent, to celebrate the tenancy of the Vicomte du Barré. Nor is there one on the wall of No 9, where a most eccentric character lived from 1768 until 1774.* He was one of the Crescent's earliest residents, and he sold his house just before the great project was completed. His name was Philip Thicknesse.

He was a soldier of fortune who longed for wealth and recognition, and was prepared to follow almost any path that would lead him to either. He tried blackmail and extortion, and was imprisoned for three months for seriously libelling an army colonel. He tried the army and authorship, with only moderate success. And he tried marriage, leading three brides hopefully to the altar; the first union was short-lived and disastrous, the second produced a reasonable dowry, and the third brought him happiness. In the final analysis he had little reason to grumble.

He was an aggressive, ill-tempered man with an inordinate capacity for making enemies. Few of his contemporaries had a good word to say about him, and some were openly abusive in their condemnation of his behaviour. One of the many with whom he quarrelled was the actor and playwright Samuel Foote, who described him as having 'the stupidity of an owl, the vulgarity of a blackguard, the obdurate heart of an assassin and the cowardice of a dunghill cock'. I always thought owls were supposed to be wise, and that cocks, whether from dunghills or more salubrious parts of the farmyard, were redoubtable fighters; but in any case, Foote's invective went too far. Thicknesse's faults were legion and his ambition, together with his irascibly quarrelsome nature, led him

---

*There is evidence to suggest that Thicknesse took the twenty-eighth house in the Crescent. The houses were not numbered until about 1800, so positive identification is difficult; but the twenty-eighth house was one of the last to be completed ,and Thicknesse's biographer, Philip Gosse, tells us that he bought his house in 1768, only a year after Wood commenced building the Crescent. No 9, one of the earlier houses to be completed, therefore seems the likelier possibility.

into an endless succession of unpleasant situations. Yet he was capable of kindness; and his memoirs reveal a sympathy for the oppressed and the underprivileged that was far from common in the age in which he lived. John Nichols, in his *Literary Anecdotes*, describes him as 'a man of probity and honour, whose heart and purse were always open to the unfortunate' — a verdict that would appear to make nonsense of Foote's vitriolic outburst.

In 1740, when he was twenty-one, he obtained a commission as Captain-Lieutenant in Brigadier Jeffries' Marine Regiment of Foot — an appointment that gave him the opportunity to wear a dashing uniform, but did little to enhance his meagre financial resources. Hopefully, he married an heiress, Maria Lanove, the daughter of a wealthy Huguenot refugee; but her dowry proved to be disappointingly small, and Thicknesse, typically, failed to endear himself to her mother. His cherished dreams of easily-acquired wealth appeared to be as remote as ever.

He first settled in Bath in 1749, with his wife and their three children. Shortly afterwards Maria and two of the children died in a diphtheria epidemic, and Thicknesse himself was taken ill. He had written to his mother-in-law requesting her to come to Bath and nurse his stricken family, but Madam Lanove had refused; and after the triple bereavement his exasperation and anger exploded in a short, bitter note that he sent to her. 'Madam' he wrote, 'Your daughter is dead, your grandchildren are dead, and I apprehend I am dying; but if I ever recover, the greatest consolation I can have is that now, I have no more to do with you'.

Three years later he married again. Lady Elizabeth Touchet was the daughter of the Earl of Castlehaven, and she brought with her a dowry of £5000 — a factor that Thicknesse must undoubtedly have taken into account at the outset: he was perennially short of money. With part of the dowry he purchased the Governorship of the Landguard Fort at Harwich, a military sinecure that helped, in a small way, to fulfil his yearning for eminence of some kind. The fort, built by Charles I in 1728, stood at the mouth of Harwich Harbour, and was garrisoned by old soldiers and service invalids. For the privilege of commanding them, Thicknesse paid £1200.

Lady Elizabeth bore him two sons and three daughters, the eldest boy becoming heir to the barony of Audley — an ironical circumstance that infuriated Thicknesse beyond measure. She died in March, 1762, at the age of thirty-seven, some six months after the birth of her last child. During the weeks preceding her death she was nursed by a close friend, Miss Ann Ford, who had joined the family in East Anglia especially for this purpose. Six months after Lady Elizabeth's death, in September 1762, Miss Ford became the third Mrs Thicknesse.

The marriage was a successful one. Like Elizabeth Linley, Ann Ford was beautiful — Gainsborough's portrait provides ample evidence of this fact — and she sang like an angel. She was also a talented performer on the viol da gamba, a stringed instrument very much like the modern violincello; and a noble lord who knew her later in Bath, was heard to remark that 'she is excellent in music, loves solitude, and has immeasurable affection'. A good deal of that affection was bestowed on Thicknesse; and after his death she wrote, perhaps with more loyalty than judgment, that 'no man was his enemy whose friendship was worth coveting'.

Among those whose friendship he certainly valued was Gainsborough, whom he met during the period of his governorship of the Landguard Fort at Harwich. Gainsborough was living in Ipswich at that time, and struggling to establish himself as a painter. Thicknesse, if he himself is to be believed, recognised the young man's genius immediately, and persuaded him that Bath was an ideal place in which to make his name and fortune. The advice was sound, and Gainsborough took it. He arrived in Bath in 1759, and soon achieved considerable success as a portrait painter.

Thicknesse returned to the city with his third wife in 1768, and took one of the new houses in the Crescent: it was No 9, and must have been very recently completed when he acquired it. He still maintained a close friendship with Gainsborough, who now lived and worked in the Circus, and continued to do everything in his power to further the artist's progress. But then, perhaps inevitably, they quarrelled. Gainsborough had painted a splendid portrait of the third Mrs Thicknesse, and had undertaken to paint Thicknesse himself. The portrait was never completed, and the irascible Thicknesse made no attempt to disguise his anger; he berated the artist in public at every opportunity, and in 1774 Gainsborough packed his bags, and left Bath permanently for London. It was a wise move professionally, of course; but there can be little doubt that it was originally prompted by the quarrel.

In that same year Thicknesse sold his house in the Crescent to 'a lady of quality' for £2000, and took a cottage behind Lansdown Place called St Catherine's Hermitage. During alterations to the cottage, one or two very ancient coffins were unearthed by the builders, and Thicknesse, with typically misguided enthusiasm, identified a mouldering skeleton in one of them as that of 'a beautiful Saxon virgin'. His nature was oddly contradictory throughout his whole life; he was, if one can imagine such a hybrid, a bitter optimist.

He wrote extensively at this time, still quarrelled regularly, and travelled in Europe whenever he could. Among his literary effusions were three volumes of revealing memoirs, and *The New Prose Bath Guide*, a factual description of the city which he hoped might rival Anstey's work in popularity. It was not a great success; but it bears the unmistakable stamp of his eccentricity, and it can still be read with enjoyment today.

His health was variable, and all his life he suffered from gallstones, taking massive doses of laudanum to alleviate the pain. Like so many of his contemporaries he was something of a hypochondriac, lending a willing ear to the claims of a wide variety of panaceas and nostrums. He even believed, like many others, that the breath of young women was helpful in prolonging life. In 1779 he wrote: 'I am myself turned of sixty, and in general, though I have lived in various climates, and suffered severely both in body and mind, yet having always partaken of the breath of young women, wherever they lay in my way, I feel none of the infirmities which so often strike the eyes and ears in this great city of sickness (he was referring to Bath) by men many years younger than myself.'

He survived for another thirteen years, although there is no evidence to suggest that the breath of young women continued to sustain him. Then, in 1792, at the age of seventy-three, he undertook another journey to France and Italy. The carriage in which he was travelling was in the neighbourhood of Boulogne when he collapsed suddenly, and died in his wife's arms.

It was perhaps typical of Thicknesse's recklessness that he had chosen to travel through France at the height of the Revolution.

Immediately after his death Ann was arrested, presumably because she appeared to be an aristocrat; eventually she was released, after establishing her identity satisfactorily. She returned to England and moved to London, staying for many years with a friend in Edgware Road, and writing a novel called *The School for Fashion*, which was published in 1800. She died in 1824 at the age of eighty-seven.

# VII    Fanny Sage and Mrs Montagu

Ann Ford, the third Mrs Thicknesse, was a beautiful woman and a talented musician. So, too, was Elizabeth Linley. Both were painted by Gainsborough, and both lived in the Crescent in the early 1770s: They were close neighbours at No 9 and No 11. And when they left, Elizabeth eloping with Sheridan in 1772 and Ann departing, two years later, with her cantankerous husband to live in Lansdown, there could well have been several residents who felt a twinge of sadness at their going. They were both attractive women, in their appearance and in their respective natures, and they must surely have been missed; although it seems unlikely that tears were shed over Thicknesse's departure.

A little more than a decade later, however, another young woman of outstanding physical beauty, and blessed with abundant charm, was adorning the Crescent's lively social scene. She lived for some time at No 20, which was the home of her uncle, the Rev Thomas Sedgwick Whalley D.D. Her name was Fanny Sage, and her grace and good looks won her the unofficial title of 'Queen of Bath'.

Dr Whalley was a typical product of the late eighteenth century — a well-educated divine, with enough money to enjoy his abundant leisure, and to indulge his taste for travel. Born in 1746, he was educated at Charterhouse and Cambridge, where he took holy orders. In 1774 he married a lady who brought him a considerable fortune, and two years later he was able to buy one of the recently completed houses in the Crescent — No 20.

Fanny Burney, whose letters were as gossipy as Horace Walpole's, met him there, and later described him as 'a young man who has a house in the Crescent, and is one of the best supporters of Lady Miller's vase at Batheaston.* He is immensely tall, thin and hand-

---

*Lady Miller achieved much acclaim at this time by instituting a weekly poetry competition at her home at Batheaston, near Bath. Guests were invited to compose a short poem on a given subject, and these were ceremonially deposited in a venerable urn that the hostess and her husband had brought back from Italy: it was said to have been owned by Cicero. The poems were taken from the urn, one by one, and read aloud; and the writer of the most successful piece was

*J. C. Nattes' view of the Crescent from the west, 1805, showing Brock Street and a glimpse of The Circus; W. Watts' elegant engraving, 1819 shows how impressive The Royal Crescent must have appeared when viewed from the River Avon.*

*Christopher Anstey—author of* The New Bath Guide, *who lived in the Crescent for twenty-two years. An earlier portrait by Hoare hangs in the magnificent Banqueting Room of the Guildhall at Bath. Portrait: William Hoare.*

some, but affected, delicate, and sentimentally pathetic; and his conversation about his own "feelings", about amiable motives, and about the wind which, at the Crescent, he said, in a tone of dying horror, "blew in a manner really frightful", diverted me the whole evening'.

Dr Whalley was not entirely dependent on his wife's fortune. When he was in his middle twenties, the Bishop of Ely presented him with the living of Hagworthingham in Lincolnshire, and then conveniently added a proviso that he need not live there, because the climate would be injurious to his health. He retained the living for more than fifty years, and the duties and responsibilities attached to it were carried out by a curate. It was a very convenient arrangement indeed.

The even tenor of his days in Bath, however, was grievously disturbed in 1778 when his favourite sister, Mrs Sage, died suddenly at the age of thirty-three; she had just returned from India where her husband, Isaac Sage, was Paymaster-General in Lord Clive's army. Whalley immediately invited her only daughter, Fanny, to share his home, and she was to enjoy his deep affection until the day he died.

Thus another beauty arrived in the Crescent. Like her predecessors, Fanny was gifted musically: she sang well, and was no mean performer on the harpsichord. Romney painted a full-length portrait of her. She was known and liked, not only in the Crescent, but in other fashionable parts of the city, and she carried her unofficial title, 'Queen of Bath', easily and well.

Inevitably, of course, there were waspish comments from less well-endowed ladies. Among Dr Whalley's numerous correspondents was a Miss Penelope Sophia Weston, whose genteel prose did little to hide her censorious feelings. 'Has our lovely Fanny made any new conquests' she wrote, dipping her pen in diluted vitriol, 'And may I dare to drop a hint that I wish you would not let

---

crowned with a chaplet of myrtle. Then, as a contemporary wrote, 'the most sensible feature of the gala, a gentle collation, concluded the business'. The poems were invariably banal; Johnson and Walpole ridiculed the whole exercise, and Fanny Burney dismissed Lady Miller as 'a round, plump, coarse-looking dame of about forty'. But the *soirées* were extremely popular, and very often there were as many as fifty carriages drawn up in front of the Batheaston house. Anstey was a frequent guest on these occasions, and so was Dr Whalley.

her run so much about Bath in a morning? Walking is certainly good for her health, and necessary; but the misfortune of Bath is that young people cannot take the advantage of exercise without being too much exposed to observation. Fanny is too attractive not to be much sought after, but she should not be too easily or frequently found. When you and Mrs Whalley think she is walking in the Crescent, she is often flying all over the Parades. The dear thing is wonderfully prone to flirtation, and hunts after a new beau who has happened to strike her fancy, with a degree of activity and interest more natural than fit'.

In the summer of 1783 Mr and Mrs Whalley let their house in the Crescent, and travelled extensively in Europe, living for much of the next two years in France, Belgium and Italy, and paying only occasional visits to Bath. Fanny continued to live in the house, but her appearances, either on the Crescent or on the Parades, became fewer; she married, and occasionally spent time with her uncle in Brüssels or Versailles. In 1828 she was widowed, and living in France, at La Flèche on the Loire. Whalley heard that she was in financial difficulties, and although he was now eighty-two and very frail, he made the difficult journey to see her; it was too much for him, and he died a few weeks after reaching her. Fanny's subsequent fate is unrecorded. No doubt Whalley eased her financial burdens and perhaps enabled her to live the remainder of her life in reasonable comfort. But the halcyon days when she had Bath at her feet must have seemed very, very far away.

On the outbreak of war in 1939, the British Boxboard Agency was evacuated to Bath, and established its headquarters at No 20 the Crescent. Several years later the agency published a pamphlet describing its occupancy of the house, in which the following appeared: 'During those years an illuminated notice hung in the Managing Director's room, with the following inscription: "Fanny Sage, known for her beauty as Queen of Bath, lived here in 1787" '. The writer went on to add that enquiries had failed to elicit any further information on Miss Sage, but that two or three fine, full-length mirrors in the hall and on the first floor landing, were perhaps associated with her stay there. If that were so, it isn't too difficult to imagine Fanny pirouetting in front of one of them, checking the line of a new dress, or adjusting her bonnet, before flying off to the

Parades. With, of course, a cautionary word from Dr Whalley echoing in her ear.

\* \* \*

Until the decline of Bath's popularity early in the nineteenth century, the Royal Crescent was a fashionable and popular promenade. On fine days both residents and visitors took gentle exercise along its curved pavement, and at weekends during the season it was thronged with well-dressed strollers. It was a colourful scene: smart barouches clattered over the cobbled roadway, haughty gentlemen on splendid horses trotted slowly by, elegantly-garbed women chatted with friends, or walked serenely on the arms of their escorts. It was a provincial microcosm of Hyde Park, Rotten Row and Kensington Gardens, and Fanny Sage knew it well. She knew, too, many of the promenaders, and must certainly have been aware of a titled lady who was frequently the cynosure of all eyes. Her name was Lady Betty Cobbe.

Lady Betty should not really concern us here, because she was not a resident of the Crescent: she lived at No 22, Marlborough Buildings. But she was an interesting character who became locally famous because she was said to have been involved in a most unusual ghost story. In fact, it was Lady Betty's grandmother, Lady Beresford, who encountered the ghost; Lady Betty, before her marriage, had inherited the title of Lady Beresford, and when Sir Walter Scott wrote a story about the incident, she was confused with her grandmother. She was frequently asked to describe the experience, and eventually found the whole business a source of annoyance.

Briefly, the story was this: the elder Lady Beresford awoke one night to find the ghost of an ancestor, Lord Tyrone, sitting on her bed. The apparition lectured her at some length on orthodox theology, and at one stage touched her wrist to emphasise a point. The wrist shrivelled alarmingly, and never recovered; and Lady Beresford was obliged to wear a black ribbon round it for the rest of her life, to conceal the marks of the ghost's fingers.

Lady Betty, it seems, could have dispelled much of the confusion by leaving her wrist uncovered. But this she never did, and she continued to be identified with the ghost's victim. She probably enjoyed the notoriety for a time, but there can be no doubt that it palled eventually. Later in her life she received a letter from a lady-in-waiting to Queen Charlotte, requesting full details of the story. She replied brusquely, saying that 'she presented her compliments, but was sure the Queen of England would not try to pry into the private affairs of her subjects, and she had no intention of gratifying the impertinent curiosity of a lady-in-waiting'.

The story of Lady Betty is told by her great grand-daughter, Miss Frances Power Cobbe, in a fascinating autobiography published early in this century. Miss Cobbe was born in 1822, and was a frequent visitor to Bath throughout her long life. Her mother had spent much of her childhood at No 29 the Crescent, then the home of Colonel and Mrs Champion, and was virtually their adopted daughter. She told Miss Cobbe that in this beautiful house, towards the end of the eighteenth century, most of Bath's fashionable society met regularly: Mrs Champion's Wednesday evening parties were famous. The Colonel, a great friend of Warren Hastings, had served as commander-in-chief of the troops of the East India Company, and No 29 was filled with exotic furnishings and objects from the sub-continent; according to a cynical observer at the time, he had enjoyed 'a good shake of the Pagoda tree'. There seems little doubt that he was the same Colonel Champion who was relieved of £650 by the Vicomte du Barré and Captain Rice in 1778. Probably the 'shake of the Pagoda tree' provided some compensation for that unlucky evening.

\*     \*     \*

A year after the Vicomte died in his duel with Captain Rice, a wealthy lady in her late fifties took possession of the centre house in the Crescent. She was Elizabeth Montagu, a vivacious, attractive woman whose life spanned almost the whole of the eighteenth century; she was born in 1720, and died in 1800. When she was twenty-one she married Edward Montagu, a grandson of the first Earl of Sandwich, and a man of considerable wealth who owned collieries and farms in Yorkshire and near Newcastle, and who was M.P. for Huntingdon. He was fifty-one when they wed, a gentle, scholarly man who pursued a lifelong interest in botany and mathematics. Despite the gap of almost thirty years between their ages, they loved one another devotedly; but for much of their married lives they were content to follow their own inclinations, and they often lived apart for long periods.

Throughout her life Mrs Montagu was a frequent visitor to Bath. She was famous for the genteel parties she gave, both in Bath and at her London home; the emphasis was on conversation and the guests, usually fashionable intellectuals, discussed literary and philosophical topics throughout the entire evening, sustained from time to time by a stimulating libation. Intelligent conversation, in Mrs Montagu's view, was infinitely preferable to gambling with cards or dice, which she heartily disliked: she was once heard to remark that the only questions one ever heard in Bath were, in the morning 'How d'ye do?' and in the evening 'What's trumps?'

Because of her penchant for literary *causeries*, for her dedicated efforts to replace cards with conversation, she became widely known as 'Queen of the Blue Stockings'. The origin of the term is vague; but it is generally supposed to have been inspired by a regular guest at her parties called Edward Stillingfleet, who usually appeared in blue worsted stockings because he couldn't afford the more expensive black silk ones which were conventionally correct for such gatherings. Soon, all women who presided over assemblies where scholars were welcomed were dubbed 'blue stockings'; and the term eventually passed into the language, to describe pedantic women generally.

Mrs Montagu, however, deserves to be remembered for more than the colour of a poor man's stockings. She was highly intelligent, a lively conversationalist, and an accomplished letter-writer. And many testified to her kind-heartedness and generosity, particularly the tenants of farms and estates that she inherited after her husband's death in 1775. On May Day every year, she entertained a small army of undernourished and very young chimney-sweeps to an *al fresco* meal of roast beef and plum pudding, in the garden of her London home.* The mantle of stern austerity implied by the term 'blue stocking' never really fitted her.

---

*Fanny Burney's description of this event is interesting for its prolixity: she called it 'an annual festival for those hapless artificers who perform the most abject offices of any authorised calling, in being the active guardians of our blazing hearths'.

During her many visits to Bath she stayed in Orange Court, Edgar Buildings, Gay Street, the Circus, the Crescent and Queen's Parade. In May 1779 she was living in the Circus and writing to a friend: 'I think the Crescent is the pleasantest situation, as well as the most beautiful in its form, of anything I ever beheld. To my great mortification there was not a house to be got there when I came, so I was obliged to content myself with one in the Circus'.

Living in the Circus could hardly have been a penance, one would have thought; but Mrs Montagu was a determined woman, and soon afterwards she was able to write: 'I have now got an admirable good house in the Crescent. I have a charming prospect from all my windows, a pretty garden, and everything so pleasant and convenient'. The rooms were large and commodious and this, too, pleased her. Small rooms she regarded as an abomination, as constraining as 'tight stays and strait shoes'; she needed spaciousness in her surroundings, and her Crescent house was the first in Bath to provide her with it. She entertained frequently, and Fanny Burney, Mrs Thrale, Lady Huntingdon, Anstey and Lord Lyttleton, among others, enjoyed her hospitality, and the conversation that she so assiduously engendered.

Later in 1779 she continued to enthuse about the advantages of her house. 'The beautiful situation of the Crescent' she wrote, 'cannot be understood by any comparison with anything in any town whatsoever. Immediately before the house there is a large space paved with the Bath stone, beyond there is a beautiful green lawn fenced by an iron rail, where sheep are feeding, and to this enclosure the inhabitants of the Crescent have a key, so that it serves as a general garden for walking . . .'. Two hundred years later there is little change: there are no sheep, of course, but there is still a green lawn with railings, and the residents still have keys to gain access to it. The noble façade is darkened by the grime of two centuries, but its grandeur is undiminished. If Mrs Montagu could see it now, she would be amazed by nothing except the television aerials and the motor cars.

\*     \*     \*

In 1798, towards the end of Mrs Montagu's long life, a distinguished physician took up residence at No 15 the Crescent, next door to the centre house. He was Dr John Haygarth, and he occupied the house for two years. For more than thirty years before that he had served as physician to Chester Infirmary, and he was in his late fifties when he came to Bath.

In those days the attention paid in hospital to such elementary precautions as isolation, ventilation and scrupulous cleanliness was negligible. John Haygarth was the first English doctor to appreciate their crucial importance, and to apply them rigorously. He conceived the idea, which is now universal, of separately treating fever patients in isolated wards, and Chester Infirmary adopted the principle in 1783. It seems incredible to us now, when we take hygiene in hospitals for granted, that these basic health requirements were hardly recognised two hundred years ago. Dr Haygarth was a pioneer in their implementation, and he is remembered in medical history for the vital contribution he made to the advancement of public health.

Bath has long been well provided with able doctors. Philip Thicknesse called it 'this great city of sickness'; and for nearly three hundred years the medical profession has been present, in generous and highly-qualified numbers, to wage war on ill-health and disease. In 1800, for example, there were twenty-two physicians with M.D. after their names in the city, and fourteen surgeons — and the population was a mere thirty-three thousand souls.

William Oliver, inventor of the Bath Oliver biscuit, was probably the most celebrated of all Bath's doctors. The honour of being the first physician to the Bath Hospital fell to him, and he established a formidable reputation in the city before his death in 1764. The famous Oliver biscuit was a vital factor in the dietary programmes he planned for patients who were taking the waters.

Another well-known physician to the Bath Hospital who came to the city in 1770, seven years after succeeding John Haygarth at Chester Infirmary, was William Falconer; he practised in the Circus for a great many years. His grandson, Randle Wilbraham Falconer, followed his example almost precisely. He, too, became physician to the hospital, practised in the city for more than thirty years, and was honoured with the mayoralty in 1857. The profession of medicine, it seems, was almost endemic in the Falconer family. William's son, Thomas, qualified as a doctor, but never practised; he took holy orders, and eventually won much repute as a classical scholar. He, too, lived in the Circus.

The Crescent's most notable doctor in the eighteenth century was Sir William Watson, who lived at No 23 for more than twenty years. He took one of the last houses to be completed in 1773, and lived there until 1794 — a long occupancy indeed in those days. He was a great friend of William Herschel the astronomer, and gained distinguished recognition for his medical and scientific work; he was knighted in 1796, and admitted as a Fellow of the Royal Society in the same year. He died in 1824.

*       *       *

One more famous name is associated with the Crescent in the period before the end of the century. William Wilberforce, the great philanthropist who campaigned so vigorously for the abolition of slavery, stayed at No 2 during the parliamentary recess late in 1798. His bill for abolition had just been defeated for the fourth time; it was finally carried in the House of Commons in 1804, and after twice being rejected by the Lords, it was given the royal assent in 1807.

Wilberforce was a frequent visitor to Bath, and there are bronze tablets on the walls of No 36 Great Pulteney Street and No 9 North Parade, recording his visits. His sojourn in the Crescent in 1798 was a family affair. The previous year he had married a Miss Spooner from Warwickshire at Walcot Church in Bath. A member of her family owned a house in the Crescent, and the young couple spent a winter holiday there, before Wilberforce returned to the House of Commons to renew the fierce struggle to get his abolition bill accepted.

# VIII    The Crescent in the Nineteenth Century

During the nineteenth century Bath's image changed considerably. Its fame as a fashionable resort continued for the first thirty years or so, and then began to fade steadily. By the middle of the century its palmy days were over; the brilliant frivolity of the Georgian era had been superceded by the practical realities of the Victorian age. The population of the city doubled during the century, and building development was concentrated on accommodation for residents rather than visitors. The railway, with all its significant consequences, reached Bath in 1840. Gas lighting changed the face of the streets at night, and horse-drawn trams revolutionised local transport. The sedan chair disappeared, to be replaced by the Bath chair. And the vast influx of visitors steadily diminished.

In 1840 one of Bath's magistrates, a Mr William Jeffs, addressed an eloquent letter to the mayor, outlining the evidences of what he called 'the city's declining condition'. The shops, the streets, the theatre, the people themselves, he maintained, were no longer as they once were; a blight had descended on them all. He concluded the letter with an impassioned cry from the heart: 'Oh Bath! Bath! the once joyous and happy Bath; the city of palaces, formerly the gayest of the gay, within whose circling walls were congregated the élite of all that was elegant, refined and intellectual, how hapless is thy destiny!'

In the long term his gloomy prognosis was unjustified. Bath's destiny proved to be far from hapless, and towards the end of the century, there was a marked revival in the city's popularity. Its fame as a spa was revitalised by the discovery of the Roman baths in 1878–80, and it became fashionable once more to 'take the waters' there. The huge Empire Hotel, now occupied by the Admiralty as offices, was built in 1899–1901 to help cope with an anticipated increase in the number of visitors. But there was to be no revival on the scale of the eighteenth century; the days of Bath's glory as a mecca for the fashionable and the famous were never to return.

In many ways, the residents of the Crescent during the nineteenth century reflected the changes that were taking place. Politicians and writers alternated with retired generals and wealthy businessmen, and their lives appear to have been sober and, in the main, exemplary. There were no outstanding extroverts among them to match the eccentric behaviour of Philip Thicknesse, or the gambling opportunism of the Vicomte du Barré and Captain Rice. But several of them achieved fame and distinction in their chosen professions.

Among them was a hero of Trafalgar. Admiral Sir William Hargood retired to Bath after a distinguished naval career that spanned almost sixty years, and lived at No 9 Royal Crescent from 1834 until 1839. At the time of Trafalgar he was a captain, commanding the *Belleisle*, an 80-gun ship-of-the-line under Nelson's flag. On that fateful 21st October, 1805, she was one of the first ships in action, following the flagship *Royal Sovereign* into the attack. She took a terrific pounding from the French and Spanish guns, and at one stage there were French ships ahead and astern of her, pouring a murderous succession of broadsides into her battered hull. She was completely dismasted, and collapsing sails and rigging covered her decks and several of her gunports, preventing many of her guns from being fired. A contemporary engraving shows her drifting helplessly in the heat and smoke of the battle, with a flag flying bravely from a pike attached to the jagged stump of her mainmast. More than thirty of her crew were killed, and nearly a hundred wounded. Hargood himself was knocked off his feet by a flying splinter, and badly bruised from his neck to his hip. Minutes later, however, he met the captain of Marines on the quarterdeck, and offered him a bunch of grapes; and for some little time they stood there, with the roar of cannonades around them, munching the fruit and discussing the progress of the battle.

Although she was incapable of manoeuvring, *Belleisle* succeeded in capturing a prize late in the afternoon. A Spanish ship, the *Argonaute*, drifted towards her through the smoke, and the captain of Marines took a boat over with several men, and boarded her. He returned with *Argonaute*'s second captain, who explained that the senior captain was wounded and that the few members of the crew who were still alive were below decks. *Belleisle*'s master took charge of the prize, and Hargood accepted the Spanish captain's sword, before inviting him down to his cabin for a cup of tea.

The English fleet limped to Gibraltar after the battle, and *Belleisle*, towed by the frigate *Naiad*, was the first to reach the shelter of the

58

Rock, where she was cheered to the echo by the crews of ships in the harbour. For Captain Hargood, as for all the English captains, there was deep satisfaction in victory — tempered by sadness at the loss of friends and colleagues, and by grief at the death of Nelson. News of the battle reached London a fortnight later, and on 6th November, 1805, *The Times* echoed the sentiments of the nation: 'We know not whether we should mourn or rejoice. The country has gained the most splendid and decisive victory that has ever graced the naval annals of England: but it has been dearly purchased. The great and gallant Nelson is no more'.

Hargood was promoted admiral on 22nd July, 1831, and two months later, on the occasion of William IV's coronation, he was awarded the KCB. He had served as a lieutenant with the King — then Prince William Henry — on the frigate *Hebe* in 1785, and afterwards they had corresponded regularly; the award was a gesture of friendship from one old salt to another, but richly deserved, nonetheless. After a three-year spell as commander-in-chief at Plymouth, Sir William spent five years of retirement in Bath, and died at No 9 Royal Crescent on 11th September, 1839. He was buried in Bath Abbey, and his portrait hangs in the famous Painted Hall at Greenwich.

If Admiral Hargood's contribution to the welfare of England was exemplary, so too was that of Sir Francis Burdett, who lived at No 16 from 1814 until 1822. He was an ardent champion of electoral reform, at a time when it was crucially needed, and he worked tirelessly throughout his life to expose abuses of power wherever he encountered them. As a baronet whose favourite recreation was fox-hunting, he seems an unlikely standard-bearer for such nineteenth-century ideals as prison reform and freedom of speech; but he served two terms of imprisonment for his outspoken views, and was heavily fined. He never lacked the courage and determination to challenge corruption in public affairs; in 1809, when the Duke of York was involved in the unsavoury business of bartered army commissions, he seconded the motion in the House of Commons for an enquiry into the Duke's behaviour. He was M.P. for Westminster then, and represented the constituency for thirty years. No politician of his day had greater integrity.

His daughter, Angela Georgina, inherited her father's deep

concern for social reform. She lived at No 16 for the first eight years of her life and later, as Baroness Burdett-Coutts, became celebrated for her great philanthropy. Hundreds of worthy causes benefited from her generosity. She administered several charities, built and endowed St Stephen's, Westminster, and other London churches and, as a lifelong lover of animals, gave active support to the work of the RSPCA. At her instigation, sewing and cookery were introduced into the curricula of elementary schools; and she even helped the costermongers of Bethnal Green in East London, by providing stables for their donkeys.

She was, of course, immensely wealthy; as a grand-daughter of Thomas Coutts, the celebrated banker, she was known as 'the richest heiress in England'. Later, she added his name to her own, and in 1871 she was raised to the peerage, in recognition of her invaluable work. She was an indefatigable hostess, and there were few outstanding figures of the day who did not share the hospitality of her table; she was intimate with the royal family, the Duke of Wellington, Sir Robert Peel, Disraeli, Gladstone, Dickens, Sir Henry Irving and many others. She died in 1906 at the age of 92, and was buried in Westminster Abbey.

The Crescent has been the home, at varying periods of their lives, of several talented women. Elizabeth Linley and Ann Ford were accomplished singers and musicians, and Fanny Sage was similarly gifted; Mrs Montagu was a prolific and informative letter-writer and a famous hostess; and the generous benefactions of Baroness Burdett-Coutts helped to make her one of the outstanding women of the nineteenth century. Another lady who lived in the Crescent during the 1830s, achieved a modest distinction in a very different sphere: she was said to have received a proposal of marriage from Napoleon, and to have turned him down.

She was Miss Marianne Hare, and she lived with her sister Caroline at No 21. They were the daughters of Mrs Henrietta Henckel Hare who originally owned the house, and who died in 1826. Marianne was wealthy; early in her life she had inherited £60,000, and about the end of the eighteenth century she had travelled extensively in Europe with her mother and Caroline. Both sisters were then young women, and it was at this time that Marianne met Napoleon in Paris. The man who was later to become the scourge of Europe was a young, impoverished artillery officer on half-pay, seriously considering marriage as a means of furthering his military career. He had yet to meet Josephine Beauharnais, and it was perfectly feasible for him to have sought the hand of a wealthy young Englishwoman. In her diary Marianne claimed that he proposed marriage to her, that she had declined, and that she regretted it bitterly afterwards. She met him later in Milan when he was at the height of his power, and he apparently treated her with warmth and great cordiality.

In 1795, however, when the proposal was made, Napoleon was ready to wed the first woman of rank and wealth who would help him on in the world; he even considered marrying an elderly lady of nearly seventy, who was reputed to have a fortune of more than a million francs. Perhaps Marianne received cautious advice from her mother.

Her nephew, the author and artist Augustus William Hare, stayed for some time at the house in the Crescent, as a child in 1839. Later in life he remembered the two elderly ladies — he called them 'the Bath aunts' — and their excessively quarrelsome natures. No doubt he was told about the Napoleon episode at that time; he referred to it briefly in a massive, six-volume autobiography that he published in 1896–1900.

He occasionally returned to Bath to visit his father's friend, the poet Walter Savage Landor, who lived at 35 St James's Square. Landor had been driven from Florence, where he had a house, by his wife's violent temper. He lived alone in Bath, but gained some consolation from the company of an attractive young woman called Miss Fray, who often came to dine with him. Her visits sometimes coincided with those of Hare, and after dinner Landor would say 'Now Augustus, I'm going to sleep — so make love to Miss Fray'. Marianne, one suspects, would have been shocked had she been alive, and able to be present. But Mr Landor would undoubtedly have enjoyed her Napoleon story.

One further distinction can be claimed for No 21, the house in which the Hare sisters lived; it probably holds the record for the shortest tenancy in the Crescent's long history. In late April 1942, Mary Ellen, Countess of Berkeley, took possession of the house. She moved in on the day before the Germans commenced their 'Baedeker' raids on Bath. That night she sheltered in the basement as the bombs whistled down; and the following morning she moved out — permanently.*

\* \* \*

Throughout the latter half of the nineteenth century, the Crescent became a haven for quite a number of retired major-generals, vice-admirals and high-ranking clergy. Its peaceful atmosphere was well suited to leisurely retirement, and senior officers who had served for many years in remote corners of the Empire, found its houses comfortably spacious and its situation salubrious. There were still those, however, who took houses there for short periods; Lord Bulwer-Lytton, the novelist and dramatist, stayed at No 9 in 1866, the year in which he was created a peer. He was in his early sixties then, and his most celebrated novel *The Last Days of Pompeii* had been written thirty years previously. The following year, 1867, he transferred his allegiance to No 2 Pulteney Street, which was then Stead's Hotel; there is a bronze plaque on the wall commemorating his visit. He returned there often during the few years preceding his death in 1873. Like many others, he seemed to find a particular solace in Bath during the closing years of a busy life.

This was certainly true of Thomas Falconer, who took No 18 the Crescent in 1881, towards the end of a long and distinguished career as a County Court judge. His family was very well known in Bath; both his father and grandfather lived in the Circus for many years, and his younger brother was a well-known doctor in the city. Falconer himself became a barrister, and at the age of forty-five he was appointed by the Earl of Elgin, Governor-General of Canada, as an arbitrator when the boundaries of Canada and the province of New Brunswick were being decided in 1850. A year later, his growing reputation won him the post of Colonial Secretary of Western Australia. He resigned before taking up the appointment, and shortly afterwards was made a County Court judge for the counties of Glamorgan and Brecknock in South Wales — a position he held for thirty years. At the age of seventy-five he came back to the city of his birth, to spend his last days in the tranquil atmosphere

---

*The raids killed 417 people in Bath, and some 1900 premises were damaged or destroyed. Two houses in the Crescent — Nos 2 and 17 — were badly damaged.

of the Crescent. Sadly, his retirement was too brief: he died only a few months later, after falling heavily during a visit to the Bath Rose Show in August, 1882.

Falconer was the second son of the Rev Thomas Falconer who qualified as a doctor, took holy orders, and lived for years in the Circus. As barrister and judge, he worked prodigiously hard. Always a staunch liberal, he fought abuses, political and social, with as much energy as Sir Francis Burdett before him. He travelled widely, and was a member of the Royal Geographical Society and the Geological Society. In Bath, he was known and admired for his own considerable achievements, as well as for those of his illustrious family.

Fourteen years after Falconer died at No 18 the Crescent, an elderly man whose name was known and acclaimed throughout the English-speaking world, took up residence in the house next door — No 17. He was Sir Isaac Pitman, who once described his own considerable achievements as 'services to the English language in giving it the briefest written form'.

He was not the first man to recognise the immense potential of shorthand; Samuel Taylor had published *An Essay intended to establish . . . an universal System of Stenography* in 1786. Pitman was able to adapt the principle, and to produce a much more practical and sophisticated method that found wide acceptance. As a young schoolmaster at Wotton-under-Edge in Gloucestershire, he had invented a system of phonography, or writing by sound, in 1837. He developed this, and with Taylor's basic principles to guide him, he finally produced the famous shorthand system that was to make such a vital impact, particularly in the worlds of commerce and journalism.

Pitman came to Bath in 1839, and lived at No 5, Nelson Place for four years. He loved the city, and at that time he wrote 'Of the many beautiful cities in this fair country, Bath is unquestionably the most beautiful'. Like Falconer before him, he came to the Royal Crescent late in his life; he was seventy-six when he took up residence at No 12, and seven years later, in 1896, he moved to No 17. Shortly afterwards he died, at the age of eighty-four, on 22nd January, 1897.

Throughout his life he was a man of regular habits and unshake-able convictions. A London newspaper described him as 'Teetotaller,

63

vegetarian, Swedenborgian, anti-vaccinationist, non-smoker, spelling reformer, and inventor of phonography. At 84 he was still working hard at his desk at 6.30 every morning, summer and winter'. He was indeed a relentless worker. In 1895, a year after he was knighted, a journalist arranged an interview with him at No 12 the Crescent, with a view to writing an article on 'Sir Isaac Pitman at Home'. The article duly appeared in a periodical called *The Young Man*; Pitman was eighty-three at the time, so the piece was clearly meant to extol the virtues of a long life dedicated to unremitting industry. 'I had been talking with Sir Isaac in his handsome dining-room' the journalist wrote, 'but I wished to see him in his own special sanctum, and he kindly led the way to what I should call a "study", but he prefers the designation of "office"; "I do not study" he said, "I only work" . . . Well-filled book-cases covered every available inch of the room. Above the book-cases are the seven cartoons of Raphael, and over the largest book-case is a bust of Milton. Phonetic literature lies in piles on the tables and floor, but there is no disorder . . . Directly Sir Isaac enters his office it seems that he must sit down to his table to write, and it is deeply interesting to note the . . . swiftness with which his pen moves across the paper . . .'.

His life was one of complete fulfilment. The day before he died, he wrote a brief note to the Rev Gordon Drummond, Minister of the New Church at Bath. It read 'To those who ask how Isaac Pitman passed away, say, Peacefully, and with no more concern than in passing from one room to another, to take up some further employment'. As his own valedictory message, it could hardly have been more appropriate.

*Mrs Sheridan—her beauty was universally acclaimed, and as Elizabeth Linley she won widespread fame as an accomplished singer. She died at the tragically early age of thirty-eight. Portrait: Thomas Gainsborough.*

*Richard Brinsley Sheridan — author of* The School for Scandal *and* The Rivals:
*in his later years he became a prominent politician, and a close friend of the Prince of
Wales. He eloped with Elizabeth Linley from No 11 Royal Crescent, on the evening of
18th March, 1772. Portrait: J. Russell 1788.*

*Philip Thicknesse — author, soldier, irascible eccentric, he claimed to have persuaded Gainsborough to settle in Bath. Portrait : William Hoare.*

*Ann Ford, the third Mrs Thicknesse — a noble lord who knew her at Bath remarked that 'she is excellent in music, loves solitude, and has immeasurable affection'. Portrait: Thomas Gainsborough c. 1760.*

# IX   The Crescent in the Twentieth Century

As in many historic buildings, a sense of continuity and permanence has pervaded the Royal Crescent for more than two hundred years. Throughout the whole of that time the colonnaded façade has retained its impressive dignity, unimpaired except for minor changes in the fenestration. The lawn still affords residents the pleasure of a quiet, open space, and they still gain access to it with a personal key, exactly as they did when Mrs Montagu lived there in 1779. Even the cobblestones in the roadway are the original ones, laid when the Crescent was built.

This semblance of a continuing pattern can occasionally be discerned in the life styles of some of the residents. Philip Thicknesse's wife, Ann Ford, was a beautiful woman, endowed with considerable musical talent, and in much the same mould as Elizabeth Linley. Sir Isaac Pitman, like Thomas Falconer, elected to spend the last days of his life in the Crescent, at the end of a busy and exceptionally distinguished career. And at the beginning of the twentieth century Frederic Harrison, equally distinguished and equally venerable, emulated them both; when he came to live at No 10 in 1912, he was eighty-one years of age, and the honours and responsibilities that had been heaped upon him during his long life, bore eloquent testimony to his great qualities as a lawyer, and as a prolific writer on historical and literary subjects. He had served on the Royal Commission on Trade Unions in 1867–69, as an alderman on the first London County Council in 1888, and as a vice-president of the Royal Historical Society. He had been a professor of juris-prudence and international law to the Inns of Court, was Rede's Lecturer at Cambridge in 1900, Washington Lecturer at Chicago in 1901, and Herbert Spencer Lecturer at Oxford in 1905. And honorary degrees had been conferred on him by the universities of Oxford, Cambridge and Aberdeen. He was a writer and thinker of very considerable stature.

Harrison was the son of a prosperous London merchant whose country residence was Sutton Place, Guildford — the impressive mansion that was later to become the home of millionaire Paul Getty. He was called to the bar by Lincoln's Inn, after becoming a fellow of Wadham College, Oxford, and practised as a lawyer for fifteen years. But writing gradually dominated his life; he published his first book in 1862, when he was thirty-one, and for nearly sixty years after that, his output was considerable and varied. He once wrote 'I fear my life has been far too dispersive, and I should have been more useful had it been concentrated on a single, or fewer interests, but I never could tear myself away from any honourable and spontaneous expression of true human nature'.

His religious beliefs were centred on the doctrine of positivism, the philosophical system of Auguste Comte which recognises only matters of fact and experience: it has been defined, perhaps less explicitly, as 'a reorganisation of life, at once intellectual, moral and social, by faith in our common humanity'. Harrison was a sincere advocate of positivism although, as a religion, it never met with wide acceptance.

Like Falconer and Pitman, he loved Bath. Two years after taking his house in the Crescent, he wrote an article on the city that was published in the *Cornhill Magazine*. 'Which of English cities is the most beautiful' he eulogised, ' — if, by beauty, we include not only fine architecture and historic buildings, picturesque site, quaint old-world labyrinths and hillsides, pure air, bright sky, with a minimum of smoke, steam, crowd and roar: above all, with an infinite variety of verdant landscape opening to the eye, far and near, high above us on every side, and brightening every street at every turn? This is indeed the special prerogative of Bath, which caused Savage Landor to compare Bath to his equally beloved Florence. Here are, first, the most important Roman buildings in our island; one of our great mediaeval cathedrals; the best English examples of Palladian architecture adapted to city planning; a river valley that may hold its own beside the Thames at Marlow, and downs that may challenge the racecourse at Goodwood'.

He went on to discuss the Crescent. 'Wood's special gift as an artist,' he wrote, 'the impression of dignity and repose, is carried to its highest point in what is known as the Royal Crescent. This building, which is not a crescent, a segment of a circle, but a segment of a very long ellipse, more than 600 feet from end to end, is remarkable for its vast size and its grand colonnade — which surpasses the scale of any similar work in England, or perhaps in Europe'.

That article appeared in April, 1914. A year later, his youngest son was killed in action in France, and his wife died in June, 1916, within four years of their golden wedding. It was a grievous war for him, as it was for countless others. But on his ninetieth birthday, 18th October, 1919, a remarkable tribute was paid to him — a tribute that must have warmed his heart considerably. An appreciative address was presented to him in his library at No 10 the Crescent — signed by the Prime Minister, Mr Lloyd George, the leaders of both the Liberal and Labour parties, the bishops of London and Exeter, the leaders of the Free Churches, and many prominent doctors, authors, journalists, artists and musicians. There were ninety signatures on the address — one for every year of his age. It was an impressive indication of the high regard in which he was held; and a month later, on 23rd November, 1919, Bath endorsed the tribute by presenting him with the freedom of the city he loved so much. His long, immensely productive life ended peacefully in mid-January, 1923.

One of Harrison's greatest friends during his last years was Professor George Saintsbury, who lived at No 1A the Crescent, the small house attached to the return frontage of No 1. The house links No 1 to the building on the corner of Upper Church Street, originally a farmhouse that had been standing for fifty years when work on the great project commenced; the two-storied link was built sometime during the nineteenth century.

George Saintsbury was yet another elderly man who came to live in the Crescent towards the end of his life: he was seventy-one when he took the little house attached to No 1 in 1916. He had recently retired as Professor of English Literature at the University of Edinburgh, and his reputation as a scholar and a man of letters was formidable. He was a prodigious reader, and it was said of him that he had read more books from more countries than any other man of his time. Arnold Bennett read his exhaustive *History of the French Novel* and commented in his journal: 'Very prolix, and bursting with subordinate sentences and clauses . . . . The amount of this old man's reading is staggering'. His literary output, too, was impressive. Writing about Saintsbury in his *Figures in Modern Literature*, J. B. Priestley says 'Note, first, the sheer bulk of his work: several volumes of essays on individual writers, periods, styles, and what not; anthologies and various editing work; biographies, histories of English,

French and European literatures; histories of criticism, English
prosody, English prose rhythm; the novel, English and French; and
so forth. The list is amazing: the mere sight of it intimidates one
and makes the more indolent of us wonder what we do with our
time'.

After taking his degree at Merton College, Oxford, Saintsbury
taught at Manchester Grammar School and Elizabeth College in
Guernsey. Then he undertook a spell of journalism with the old
*Saturday Review*, producing innumerable articles and reviews that
were outstanding for their scholarship and perceptive insight, before
taking up his post at Edinburgh. He came to Bath during the first
world war, and lived for sixteen years in the Crescent; during that
time his venerable head, crowned with a black skull cap and fringed
with a long white beard, could always be seen through the ground
floor window of his study, as he pored over a book or a manuscript.
Before infirmity confined him indoors, he could often be recognised on his morning walks, carrying a string bag full of books, and
strolling down to Grand Parade; like Lord Rosebery and Rudyard
Kipling, he considered the view across the river and over the valley
from there to be outstanding.

He was never a public figure in the city, and he always declined
invitations to sit on committees, or accept presidencies. In 1925 a
local editor suggested to him that he might be prepared to give an
interview and supply a photograph to the paper, on the eve of his
eightieth birthday. The old man's reply was short and very definite.
'Dear Sir' he wrote, 'I am sorry to refuse your request. But I have
not given, and am not giving or intending to give, any photo etc for
interview etc to any newspaper in respect of the celebration of my
birthday. So I hope you will not consider my refusal uncivil. Yours
faithfully . . .'.

He loved wine as well as literature, and in 1920 he published
*Notes on a Cellar Book*, a delightful and informative summary of his
own long experience as an imbiber, that has been reprinted several
times. And in the twenties he had the unusual distinction of having a
club named after him: its object was 'to bring together those literary
men who, unlike Chesterton and Belloc, regard wine as a more
delectable beverage than beer'. The accolade must have delighted
him hugely.

He died, full of years and wisdom, in 1933, and the bronze tablet on the wall of No 1A perpetuates his association with Bath. In its issue of 30th January, 1933, *The Times* newspaper epitomised his achievement succinctly and admirably: 'Seldom does so ripe and so full a scholar and man leave the world of good books and companionable wine as the veteran George Saintsbury, who has just died in the Augustan peace of the Royal Crescent in Bath. . . .'

The old professor would have found it difficult to write a better epitaph himself.

* * *

Philip Thicknesse, that hopeful and industrious eccentric, referred to Bath as 'this great city of sickness'. He sincerely believed — and this could be a heartening thought for male hypochondriacs—that by inhaling the breath of young women, he could improve his health and prolong his life. He lived to be seventy-three — a good age for the eighteenth century — and could well have considered his hypothesis to be justified. More conventionally-minded observers, however, have agreed that the ambience of Bath is reasonably conducive to longevity; and never more so, it seems, than in the Royal Crescent. Consider the evidence. Christopher Anstey and Sir William Watson both celebrated their eightieth birthdays there; George Saintsbury died when he was eighty-eight; and Frederick Harrison and Sir Isaac Pitman achieved the venerable ages of ninety-three and eighty-four respectively. Admittedly, some of them came to the Crescent late in their lives; but their ultimate days were prolonged there, and spent in rewarding peace.

As I write, the pattern is continued by Mr Clifford Francis, who lives at No 5. He reached his ninety-first birthday in 1980, and after a long, active life as a colonial administrator in Fiji and the Solomon Islands, and as a high court judge in Uganda and Nigeria, he relaxes now in the gentle, undemanding atmosphere of the Crescent. After Oxford, where he was at Lincoln College, he took administrative posts in Fiji and the Solomon Islands before 1914, when conditions there would have provided a perfect setting for a Somerset Maugham short story. Soon after the first world war commenced, he joined the East Surrey Regiment, and was wounded at Ypres. Lincoln's Inn called him to the bar in 1924, and subsequently he served as a judge in the New Hebrides in the South Pacific, in Uganda, and in Nigeria, before his retirement in 1945. Like Harrison, he lost a son in action, killed in North Africa in 1941 while serving with the Royal Gloucestershire Hussars.

He came to Bath with his charming wife in 1978, primarily to be close to their daughter, who lives in Bristol. But there were other, perhaps less cogent reasons. Their three-day honeymoon in 1916 was spent in the city, at the old Spa Hotel; and he confesses to a long-felt desire to spend his last days in the Royal Crescent — just as Falconer, Pitman, Harrison and Saintsbury had elected to do before him. In itself, it is surely a tribute to Wood's timeless masterpiece that so many outstanding men have felt this strong compulsion.

The Dowager Lady Celia Noble was in the same distinguished tradition; she lived at No 22 the Crescent for many years, and died there in 1962, at the age of ninety-two. She was a grand-daughter of Isambard Kingdom Brunel, the celebrated engineer who built the Great Western Railway, and designed the revolutionary steamship *Great Eastern*. Her father, Arthur James, was an assistant master at Eton, and her mother was Brunel's daughter, Florence. After her marriage to Saxton Nobel, who later succeeded to a baronetcy, she became well known as a hostess in musical and artistic circles in London, and after she came to Bath she continued, for many years, to arrange concerts of chamber music at her home in the Crescent. Princess Marie Louise, a daughter of Queen Victoria, stayed with her whenever she came to Bath, and Queen Mary, consort of King George V, visited her frequently during the last war. Her salon was the last of a line that stretched back to Mrs Montagu in the eighteenth century.

\*       \*       \*

As the twentieth century progressed, the general pattern of life in the Crescent inevitably underwent change. In the years before the first world war many of the houses were occupied by single families, often with maids in residence and, perhaps, a chauffeur and a footman. Later, as conventional life styles altered, more and more of the houses were converted into flats and, occasionally, offices; and after the last war it was not uncommon to see several of them vacant, at prices that now seem incredibly low. In 1950, for example, it was possible to buy a Crescent house for £4000, and even before 1970 one could have been acquired for as little as £7500.

After 1970, however, values soared dramatically. In that year Mrs Rottboll, whose husband had died in 1961 after serving as Danish Consul-General in London, decided to sell No 7 — a magnificent house, then used in its entirety, with six bedrooms and three bathrooms; the anticipated price at auction was estimated at £20,000. Three years later No 9, the home of Mrs G. M. Thomasson — a lady, it was said, in the grand tradition of Crescent residents — came on to the market, and was expected to sell for £50,000. And by 1980, prospective buyers were having to consider prices in the region of £80,000 or £90,000 — and even more if a house was exceptional.

Lady Noble maintained her elegant establishment at No 22 until her death in 1962. At present the house is owned and occupied by Miss Amabel Wellesley-Colley; and apart from the addition of a lift, the interior structure has remained unchanged for more than two centuries.

Miss Wellesley-Colley is a descendant of the Duke of Wellington, and a very determined lady. Some years ago the front door of her house was painted yellow, and yellow blinds were fitted to the windows. The Bath City Council objected to this, maintaining that doors in the Crescent should be painted white, as the younger John Wood had prescribed, and that the colour of Miss Wellesley-Colley's door materially altered the appearance of a listed building; on 1st June, 1971, they issued an order that she must have the door repainted, and remove the yellow blinds. The chairman of the development committee said 'If we do not exert control, we could get reds, blues, greens and all sorts of colours detracting from the glory of the Royal Crescent. It is listed as a grade one building of historical and architectural importance. Visitors to the city have complained about the yellow, as well as people living in the Crescent'.

This was true; Brigadier Chippindell, a near neighbour, had muttered darkly to a reporter 'If I told you what I think about the yellow door, everything would fuse'. But Miss Wellesley-Colley was unabashed, and in the tradition of her noble forebear, she prepared to do battle. 'The cost of fighting the planners' she told the press, 'is appalling, and must daunt many people. But I am determined not to give in'. She maintained that the authorities had no right to dictate what colour her front door must or must not be: it was a violation of her personal freedom. An eminent QC was retained on her behalf, and a year later, in August 1972, the Secretary of the Environment, Mr Peter Walker, finally declared that the door and blinds could remain yellow. Miss Wellesley-Colley had won a famous victory.

She still talks about it with a smile. The subsequent publicity pleased her immensely, and she feels that she has become something of a tourist attraction; scores of Americans, she says, call at No 22 each summer, to chat with her about the whole affair. And the yellow door, of course, is still there — tangible and irrefutable evidence of her success.

In other, more general spheres, local residents have often protested vigorously against proposed measures that they considered to be prejudicial to their interests, or to the Crescent's image. Suggestions that the façade should be floodlit after dark, that the lawn might be advantageously used as a sculpture park, and that a swimming pool and lido should be sited on ground below the lawn, were all withdrawn after protests. One of the most surprising proposals was contained in Professor Abercrombie's report, 'A Plan for Bath', published in 1945; in addition to several far-reaching recommendations, including the provision of a new hotel and a concert hall in the centre of the city, the professor suggested that the council offices should be moved to the Royal Crescent. The plan failed to materialise, and a large number of Bath's well-wishers were able to breathe freely again.

# X  The Royal Crescent Hotel

The central house of the Crescent is No 16. It is one of the largest houses, and the adjacent Nos 15 and 14 also come into this category.

There are two distinguishing features about the façade of No 16 which emphasise its commanding position at the apex of the great semi-elliptical curve of the Crescent. Four columns are grouped in pairs, and there is an arched first-floor window from which both arms of the Crescent can be viewed in all their elegant symmetry.

The houses, as we have seen, have had some notable occupants, particularly during the first fifty years of their history. Mrs Montagu, who rejoiced in the spaciousness of their rooms, entertained many of the outstanding literary figures of the late eighteenth century there. The Duke of York, George III's second son, found the relaxing atmosphere a welcome change from the pressures of life as commander-in-chief of the British army. One of the greatest of all nineteenth-century philanthropists, Baroness Burdett-Coutts, spent eight years of her childhood in their Augustan calm. During the later nineteenth century a Mrs Elizabeth Landon occupied No 16 for more than twenty years; another long-term resident was Mr W. Jerdone Braikenridge J.P., who lived there through the closing decades of the century. The last private resident appears to have been a Mr Stanislaus Eyre.

The first dramatic change for over a hundred years came in 1950, when No 16 became a guest house, owned and managed by Mr and Mrs John Newman. In 1971, together with No 15, the guest house designation was abandoned, and the Royal Crescent Hotel was launched. During 1974 Mr and Mrs Newman sold the hotel to a local consortium, in whose hands it remained a discreet, if somewhat sleepy and neglected two-star hotel until 1978, when it was acquired by the chairman of a London club and the senior partner of a firm of city solicitors, who shared an enthusiasm for eighteenth-century architecture. Its renaissance was assured.

Mr John Tham, chairman of the London Sloane Club, had positive ideas about the restoration of the two central properties in the Crescent. All modern partitions would go; rooms were to be restored to their original dimensions; all ceilings and decorations

73

that had been damaged or changed would be renewed. No modern hotel features were to be allowed to introduce a discordant note into the eighteenth-century atmosphere of the houses — no plastic, no musac, no reception office with chattering typewriters or other paraphernalia. Victorian additions that had, over the last century, disfigured the backs of the houses, would be demolished. In short, the architects' brief was to re-create the original grandeur of Nos 15 and 16, whilst providing the comforts of a hotel that would rank with the greatest in Europe. Within twelve months of restoration work commencing, their ambitions were realised.

Nos 15 and 16 Royal Crescent have been transformed into a unique hotel, decorated and furnished in a manner that complements their eighteenth-century graciousness. To walk through the buildings today is to experience the elegance of a more leisurely age. Each room is decorated in period style; the furniture, carpets, and the pictures adorning the walls, have all been chosen with infinite care for authentic detail.

There are four suites, named after personalities connected with the Royal Crescent. The Sir Percy Blakeney suite, occupying the first floor of No 16, is not only one of the most magnificent drawing rooms in the Crescent, but it is also where Baroness Orczy's Scarlet Pimpernel is said to have entertained. After his strenuous adventures in France, it was claimed that he married and settled down at No 16 Royal Crescent.* Pride of place in this truly splendid room is given to the late seventeenth-century four-poster bed that was donated to the hotel by Mr Charles Robertson, author of *Bath: an Architectural Guide*, provided it never left No 16.

Named after the Crescent's architect, the John Wood the Younger suite has a full tester bed in a raised alcove, separated from the rest of the room by a low balustrade. It was an eighteenth-century practice for the aristocracy to receive guests whilst still in bed; and the balustrade encouraged all but the most intimate to remain at a discreet distance.

Although both the Brinsley Sheridan and the Duke of York suites have fine original stucco ceilings, the craftsmanship of the latter, with

---

*Sir Percy Blakeney was, of course, a fictitious character, the Scarlet Pimpernel of Baroness Orczy's novels about the French Revolution.

its swans, flowers and garlands in strong relief, is quite spectacular, as can be seen from the illustration. The panelled walls of the Brinsley Sheridan suite are delicate blue, and the fireplace is unmistakably Georgian. All these suites have open fireplaces, and log fires during the winter months add a final touch of realism. But, happily for guests, authenticity does not preclude the provision of those modern comforts expected by the discerning traveller.

The creative efforts of John Tham, John Lewis and their designer and architect, were acknowledged only months after the buildings were reopened, when the hotel was recognised as one of the most beautiful in Europe by the European press. Then, in November 1980, the Royal Crescent Hotel received the ultimate accolade when it was awarded the Egon Ronay Gold Plate, as Hotel of the Year for 1980 — thereby joining the illustrious group of famous hotels that have been similarly honoured, including such internationally recognised names as the Ritz and the Connaught.

A delightful feature of the hotel is its art collection, specially commissioned, and formed by Lord Crathorne. It contains several fine examples of the work of eighteenth-century artists. The entrance hall is graced by a Reynolds, and there is a Gainsborough portrait, of a young woman, in the dining room. The cartoonist, Thomas Rowlandson, is also well represented with a water-colour entitled 'The Old Tea Room, Assembly Rooms, Bath', in the drawing room; and a set of his distinctive caricatures — twelve in all, and entitled 'The Comforts of Bath' — depict the problems encountered by a gout-ridden, middle-aged squire, married to a beautiful woman, and determined to enjoy all the pleasures offered by eighteenth-century Bath. Thomas Barker of Bath considered himself to be the natural successor to Gainsborough, and his work is represented by two paintings in the bar, which is dominated by Francis Cotes' portrait of Squire Collingwood, dated 1769. Cotes' portraits are also in the National Portrait Gallery, and in the Tate.

One of the most charming pictures in the collection hangs in the dining room — a delicate water-colour, painted in 1807 by John Nixon, and entitled 'Waiting for the Bath Coach'. It is a perceptively witty impression of a motley group of travellers in the front room of a coaching inn, enduring the frustration of delay as their coach is prepared for the arduous journey to Bath. Nixon, who knew the city well, was a caricaturist in the mould of Rowlandson, and much of his work has the same light-hearted touch.

In the drawing room there is a delightful tapestry picture inscribed: 'Eliza Lucas worked at Mrs Rosco's Boarding School, Royal Crescent, Bath, in the year 1788'. And throughout the hotel there are contemporary portraits of Sarah Siddons, Lord Nelson, Gainsborough, William Pitt, Charles Dickens, and a host of others who lived in, or visited Bath. A massive contemporary portrait of George III dominates the well of the main staircase, and in the reception area hangs a water-colour by Thomas Malton, one of the most attractive views of the Crescent ever produced, and executed as early as 1788. The whole collection has been skilfully assembled, and most attractively displayed. But perhaps its most remarkable characteristic is that nearly all the oil paintings, water-colours, prints and mezzotints, numbering some one hundred and twenty works, are directly connected with the history or architecture of the city. It is truly a Bath collection.

Like most famous houses, No 15 has a ghost — last seen by Mrs Newman. Late one summer afternoon a few years ago, she was carrying a tea-tray up the Horseshoe Staircase, when she saw a lady in a long blue silk dress at the top of the stairs. Mrs Newman paused, and moved to one side; and the lady in blue swept graciously down, bestowing a warm smile on her, and disappearing completely at the bottom of the stairs.

Speculation, of course, has been rife as to the ghost's identity. My own guess is that it was Mrs Elizabeth Montagu, about to supervise the preparations for one of her famous soirées. The warm smile no doubt indicated that all boded well for the occasion, and that the guests had been well chosen — Fanny Burney, perhaps, Christopher Anstey and Dr Whalley; and the impecunious Stillingfleet.

Although not exactly as envisaged by John Wood the Younger two hundred years ago, something of the eighteenth-century's style and vigour has therefore returned, with the hotel, to the Royal Crescent — the foremost architectural expression in England of the confidence and sheer sense of enjoyment that typifies that age, and distinguishes it so clearly from the materialism of the Victorian era that was to follow.

# XI   The Crescent in Fiction

In the small cavalcade of Crescent residents that we have discussed in the preceding pages there have been some, undoubtedly, who would have added lustre to the plots of half-a-dozen works of fiction. The emotional problems of Elizabeth Linley and Sheridan have already been popularised in novel form, and Thicknesse's story has been vividly told by Philip Gosse, under the title of *Dr Viper*. But the lives of Fanny Sage, Marianne Hare, the Vicomte du Barré, Colonel Champion, Mrs Montagu and Sir Francis Burdett would all have provided rich material for an imaginative writer in search of atmosphere and plot for a historical novel.

The Crescent itself has rarely figured in English fiction. But there are, nevertheless, one or two illustrious exceptions. Dickens, Jane Austen and Henry Fielding used it as a background for incidents in their novels; and Baroness Orczy made No 16 the ultimate home of Sir Percy Blakeney, the hero of her novels about the French Revolution. He was better known in France, of course, as the Scarlet Pimpernel; and when his hair-raising exploits were finally over, the Baroness arranged a good marriage for him, and a life of genteel inactivity in the Crescent — a fitting reward for such a resourceful soldier of fortune.

Dickens was no stranger to Bath. As a young parliamentary reporter, he visited the city in the spring of 1835, to report a speech by Lord John Russell for the *Morning Chronicle*; on that occasion he stayed at the Saracen's Head in Broad Street. Later, he often visited his friend, Walter Savage Landor, at 35 St James's Square, and wrote much of *Little Dorrit* there. But it was in *Pickwick Papers* that he satirised the social life of the city, and involved his characters in a bizarre incident in the Crescent.

Mr Pickwick and his friends, Mr Tupman, Mr Snodgrass and Mr Winkle, had decided to go to Bath because, as the immortal little man said, 'none of us have been there before'. They travelled by stagecoach from London, and shared the journey with the rather formidable Mr Dowler and his wife; and after arriving in Bath, they all lodged at the old White Hart in Stall Street. During the ensuing days they explored the city, drank the waters in the Pump Room, and attended a ball at the Assembly Rooms — activities that enabled Dickens to satirise the Bath scene in much the same way that Anstey had done seventy years previously. At the ball, Mr Pickwick was introduced to the Dowager Lady Snuphanuph* and the foppish Lord Mutanhed, and was unwillingly involved in a game of whist. 'In the tea-room' wrote Dickens, 'and hovering round the card-tables, were a vast number of queer old ladies and decrepit old gentlemen, discussing all the small talk and scandal of the day, with a relish and gusto which sufficiently bespoke the intensity of the pleasure they derived from the occupation. . . . And seated on some of the back benches, where they had already taken up their position for the evening, were divers unmarried ladies past their grand climacteric, who, not dancing because there were no partners for them, and not playing cards lest they should be set down as ir-retrievably single, were in the favourable position of being able to abuse everybody without reflecting on themselves. In short, they could abuse everybody, because everybody was there.'

Mr Pickwick duly took the waters. He took a quarter of a pint before breakfast, and then walked up a hill; and another quarter of a pint, and then walked down a hill. And after every fresh glass he declared 'in the most solemn and emphatic terms, that he felt a great deal better: whereat his friends were very much delighted, though they had not been previously aware that there was anything the matter with him'. His faithful manservant, the redoubtable Sam Weller, was less enthusiastic about the experience; he thought the waters had 'a wery strong flavour o' warm flat irons'.

'The great pump-room' Dickens wrote, 'is a spacious saloon, ornamented with Corinthian pillars, a music gallery, and a Tompion clock, and a statue of Nash. . . . There are baths near at hand, in which a part of the company wash themselves; and a band plays afterwards, to congratulate the remainder on their having done so. . . . There is an immensity of promenading, on crutches and off, with sticks and without, and a great deal of conversation, and liveliness, and pleasantry'.

---

*It is said that Dickens modelled his character, Lady Snuphanuph, on the Dowager Countess of Belmore, the widow of an Irish peer, who lived at No 17 the Crescent for thirty years until her death, at the age of 86, in 1841.

Mr Pickwick decided that the party would remain in Bath for two months, and that it would be advisable for them to find private lodgings for that period; the White Hart's tariff clearly imposed too much of a strain on their collective purse. They were offered the upper part of a house in the Royal Crescent, but the accommodation was larger than they required. Mr Dowler and his wife came to the rescue, however, and took one of the bedrooms and a sitting-room; and eventually they all moved in.

One evening shortly afterwards, Mrs Dowler went to a party. Mr Dowler was feeling unwell, and decided not to go with her, although he chivalrously promised to wait up until she returned. But he dropped off to sleep; and just as the clock struck three, 'there was blown into the crescent a sedan chair with Mrs Dowler inside, borne by one short fat chairman, and one long thin one, who had had much ado to keep their bodies perpendicular: to say nothing of the chair. But on that high ground, and in the crescent, which the wind swept round and round as if it were going to tear the paving stones up, its fury was tremendous. They were very glad to set the chair down, and give a good round loud double-knock at the street door'.

Nobody answered, and after repeated knockings the house still remained silent. Just as the chairmen were losing their patience, Mr Winkle staggered downstairs in his dressing-gown, opened the door, and ventured outside on to the front step; and at that precise moment a violent gust of wind slammed the door shut. Mr Winkle's reaction was a panic-stricken one; horrified at the realisation that he was locked out in his night attire, he dashed smartly into the sedan chair, where Mrs Dowler was still seated. She 'raised a violent and dismal shriek', and Mr Dowler, who had finally appeared on the scene, assumed at once that someone was about to run away with his wife. Threatening to cut the abductor's throat from ear to ear, he chased the terrified Mr Winkle all the way round the Crescent until they reached the house once more. The door was open, and Mr Winkle dashed inside and closed it firmly; and when he reached the safety of his room, he barricaded himself in with every item of furniture that he could move. Mr Dowler bellowed more murderous threats through the keyhole; and, 'after a great confusion of voices in the drawing-room, amidst which that of Mr Pickwick was distinctly heard endeavouring to make peace, the inmates dispersed to their several bed-chambers, and all was quiet once more'.

One of Dickens' great talents as a major novelist was his uncanny ability to choose appropriate names for his characters. Scrooge and Fagin are well-known and good examples. So, too, is Pickwick; it suits the rotund, bespectacled little man perfectly. There is little doubt that Dickens encountered the name on one of his first visits to Bath. At that time, the landlord of the White Hart* was an enterprising fellow called Moses Pickwick; he operated the coach service between London and Bath, and his name was painted on the doors of all his vehicles. His great grandfather, Eleazer Pickwick, had been a foundling, saved from starvation by some compassionate soul in the village of Pickwick, near Bath, and given the name of the place where he had been found.

Dickens, as we have seen, often visited Bath to stay with Walter Savage Landor in St James's Square. Later in his life, however, he grew to dislike the city — for a reason that now seems remarkably superficial. He was present in the Assembly Rooms when Bulwer Lytton's play *Not So Bad As We Seem* was performed by the Guild of Literature. Dickens was a member of the Guild, and had given advice on certain aspects of production; and when the play was coldly received by the audience, and awarded poor notices in the local press, he was deeply displeased. He never forgave Bath from that moment.

Jane Austen lived with her family in Bath for five years, from 1801 until 1806, but she was never fond of the city. Some time after leaving it, she wrote to her sister Cassandra 'It will be two years tomorrow since we left Bath for Clifton, with what happy feelings of escape!' And perhaps she herself was speaking when, in *Northanger Abbey*, Isabella Thorpe says to Catherine Morland 'I get so immoderately sick of Bath; your brother and I were agreeing this morning that though it is vastly well to be here for a few weeks, we would not live here for millions'.

---

*The White Hart was one of Bath's oldest and most famous inns; it appears on Gilmore's map of the city published in 1694. Its situation was immediately opposite the Pump Room in Stall Street, where Arlington House now stands. It was demolished in 1869.

*Frederick Augustus, Duke of York — the second son of George III, and Commander-in-Chief of the British army. He lodged on several occasions at Nos 1 and 16, Royal Crescent. Portrait: D. Wilkie, 1823.*

*Professor George Saintsbury — a distinguished scholar and man of letters, he lived at No 1A the Crescent during the last years of a long and busy life. Portrait: William Nicholson 1923.*

There are possibly two reasons that help to explain her disenchant-
ment. She loved village life and the countryside, and when her
father, who was a rural vicar in Hampshire, declared his intention
of retiring to Bath, she was so distressed, we are told, that she 'fainted
away'. And just before the move was made her aunt, Mrs Leigh
Perrot, who lived in Bath, was accused of stealing lace from a
haberdasher's shop there. She was tried by jury at Taunton Assizes,
and acquitted. But although it seems to have been simply a shop-
lifting charge that was proved to be unjustified, its impact was
considerable; in those days, such an offence could have carried a
punishment of fourteen years' transportation. Jane, like the rest of
her family, was shocked, and the case could hardly have endeared
her to Bath.

Nevertheless, the major parts of two of her novels — *Northanger
Abbey* and *Persuasion* — are set in the city, and the life she herself
led there is perfectly mirrored in both of them. Catherine Morland,
the young heroine of *Northanger Abbey*, spends six weeks in Bath
with her friends the Allens, visits the Assembly Rooms and the
Pump Room, and joins the promenaders in the Royal Crescent on
Sundays after church. Jane herself often walked in the Crescent,
and across Crescent Fields, and at one stage in the novel she tells
how the Allens and the Thorpes 'hastened away to the Crescent to
breathe the fresh air of better company'. She clearly enjoyed strolling
there. And there were pleasant diversions to savour, as well as the
architecture and the view across the River Avon. 'Miss Irvine invited
us, when I met her in the Crescent, to take tea with them' she informed a correspondent in 1805. That long, semi-elliptical pavement
was a perfect rendezvous for the respectable ladies of Bath.

In a letter written during her first visit to the city in 1799, she
included an item of local news that seems almost to have been added
as an afterthought: 'In the morning Lady Willoughby is to present
the Colours to some Corps of Yeomanry or other, in the Crescent'.
But one hundred and eighty years later, the brief sentence acquired a
rather special topicality. On the morning of 26th October 1979,
Her Majesty Queen Elizabeth the Queen Mother stepped on to the
Crescent lawn from a red helicopter of the Queen's Flight, and later
presented new colours to the 6th Battalion of the Somerset Light
Infantry, drawn up on the lower part of the lawn. The regimental

band played, the troops marched and counter-marched with well-drilled precision, and the watching crowds applauded — exactly, no doubt, as they had played, marched and applauded nearly two hundred years previously, in the same place. The coincidence itself is unimportant. But, in a small way, it confirms the absence of radical change that still characterises the Royal Crescent to this day.

Miss Austen's last novel, *Persuasion*, was completed in 1816 at a time when Bath's popularity as a pleasure resort was beginning to fade. Houses in the higher parts of the city were then attracting retired military men and colonial officers, and one of the novel's characters, Sir Walter Elliot, takes 'a very good house in Camden Place — a lofty, dignified situation, such as becomes a man of consequence'. Sir Walter was arrogant and conceited, and Miss Austen characterised him superbly. He considered the worst aspect of Bath to be 'the number of its plain women'. And at one point in the story he stands in the doorway of a shop in Bond Street, and counts 'eighty-seven women go by, one after another, without there being a tolerable face among them'. One can visualise him perfectly. *Persuasion* contains many delightful vignettes of Bath, but Jane's enthusiasm for the Crescent must have waned a little by the time the novel was written; it plays no part in the story at all.

Tobias Smollett was another English novelist whose view of Bath was less than complimentary. His first novel, *Roderick Random*, brought him fame and recognition. But he cherished an ambition to become a successful doctor, and tried to establish a practice in Bath. He failed, and his disappointment bred bitterness; and in his last novel, *Humphrey Clinker*, published in 1770, he created a character, a testy old bachelor called Matthew Bramble, who lost no opportunity to pour scorn on the city and its fashionable visitors.

*Humphrey Clinker* is written in epistolary form and Bramble, staying in Bath, is given every chance to grumble. He complains about 'the noise, tumult and hurry'; about the sedan chairs standing in the rain, 'soaking in the open street, till they become so many boxes of wet leather'; and about 'the rage of building . . . contrived without judgement, executed without solidity, and stuck together with so little regard to plan and propriety'.

This last criticism is harsh indeed; but Bramble becomes even more uncomplimentary when he describes the Circus. 'A pretty bauble designed for shew' he sneers, 'like Vespasian's amphitheatre turned inside out'. And finally, confusing the two John Woods, he fires a last salvo at the new development generally. 'The same artist who planned the Circus' he complains, 'has likewise projected a Crescent; when that is finished, we shall probably have a Star, and those who are living thirty years hence may, perhaps, see all the signs of the Zodiac exhibited in architecture at Bath'.

Smollett's sarcasm was engendered by frustration; had he been able to join the ranks, and share the success, of Bath's fashionable doctors, Matthew Bramble, one feels, would have talked about the city in much more honeyed terms. Nevertheless, *Humphrey Clinker* is a notable example of the eighteenth-century picaresque novel, and gives Smollett a definite kinship with Henry Fielding, whose great masterpiece, *Tom Jones*, had been published a little more than twenty years earlier. Both books are characterised by exuberant humour, and a deep insight into the labyrinthine variations of human nature.

Fielding often stayed at Twerton, then near Bath, but now within the city's boundaries. To this day, *Tom Jones* remains one of the great classic novels; and many people who had never read the book were recently able to savour its earthy charm in Tony Richardson's brilliant film, which captured the novel's atmosphere completely. The phenomenal success of the film encouraged Mr Richardson to embark on a production of Fielding's first novel, *The Life and Adventures of Joseph Andrews*; and one of the scenes from the new film was shot in the Royal Crescent, in May 1976.

In choosing the Crescent as a setting, at a time when the great colonnade was nearing completion, Mr Richardson allowed himself to indulge in a little artistic licence. 'Joseph Andrews' was published in 1742, twenty-five years before the younger John Wood commenced work on his masterpiece, and Fielding could never have known of its existence: he died in 1754. But the choice was justified, because the Crescent provided a perfect eighteenth-century background. The scene, from the early stages of the novel, showed the gout-ridden Lord Booby leaving No 1, and being helped into a carriage. Scaffolding had been erected at the west end of the facade, and in the roadway there were masons chipping away at huge blocks of stone, cauldrons full of boiling tar, and lots of straw. One or two indolent-looking gentlemen trotted by on horseback, and there was even a dairymaid and a cow on the lawn to add a suitably bucolic touch. With anachronisms like television aerials and lamp-posts discreetly removed, the atmosphere was impressively authentic: and the local people who had been enrolled as 'extras' enjoyed their part in the proceedings immensely.

There was, too, a happy sequel. The film company paid a sum of several hundred pounds to compensate for the disruption that had been caused; and this enabled the residents' association of the Crescent to erect much-needed new railings round the wide expanse of the lawn.

\*     \*     \*

There is one occasion in the Bath calendar that Pickwick would have loved, and that might even have brought a grunt of approval from Matthew Bramble. Each year, as darkness falls on the first day of the Bath Festival, the residents of the Circus, Brock Street and the Royal Crescent place lighted candles in their windows. The effect is magical. The tiny flames invest the old façades with an almost ethereal beauty, and the Crescent, seen from below the lawn, looks like the auditorium of some vast and splendid opera house before the curtain goes up. One or two horse-drawn carriages clatter over the old cobblestones, and a group of madrigal singers entertains the crowds until midnight. For those two brief hours, the Royal Crescent is transformed; it becomes once more a social fulcrum, a crowded rendezvous of promenaders, strolling, gossiping and simply enjoying themselves. Perhaps the scene is more boisterous than that to which Jane Austen and Lady Betty Cobbe were accustomed. But, in a delightful way, it emphasises and perpetuates the unique charm for which Bath has long been famous — and to which the Royal Crescent has contributed so abundantly.

APPENDIX 1

# Chronology of Royal Crescent

1766   Christopher Anstey's *New Bath Guide* published
1767   Foundation stone laid
1768   Philip Thicknesse at No 9
1770   Christopher Anstey at No 4
1771   The Linley family at No 11
1772   Elizabeth Linley elopes with Sheridan
1773   Elizabeth Linley marries Sheridan in London
1773   Sir William Watson at No 23
1775   The Crescent completed
1777   Sheridan's *School for Scandal* produced in London
1778   Sheridan's *School for Scandal* produced in Bath, with Sarah
        Siddons
1778   Vicomte du Barré and Captain Rice at No 8
1778   Fanny Sage at No 20
1779   Mrs Montagu at No 16
1786   Princesse de Lamballe at No 1
1792   Philip Thicknesse dies in France
1792   Elizabeth Linley dies
1792   Christopher Anstey at Marlborough Buildings
1796   Duke of York at No 1 : later at No 16
1798   Dr John Haygarth at No 16
1798   William Wilberforce at No 2
1801   Jane Austen living in Bath
1805   Christopher Anstey dies
1814   Sir Francis Burdett and daughter (later Baroness Burdett-
        Coutts) at No 22
1830   Marianne Hare at No 21
1834   Admiral Sir William Hargood at No 9
1837   *Pickwick Papers* published
1866   Lord Bulwer-Lytton at No 9
1881   Thomas Falconer at No 18
1882   Thomas Falconer dies
1889   Sir Isaac Pitman at No 12

*Appendix 1*

1896    Sir Isaac Pitman at No 17
1897    Sir Isaac Pitman dies
1898    First bronze commemorative tablet fitted on Herschel's
        house, 19 New King Street
1912    Frederic Harrison at No 10
1916    George Saintsbury at No 1A
1923    Frederic Harrison dies
1933    George Saintsbury dies
1942    Briefest tenancy: Countess of Berkeley leaves No 21 after
        one night's stay
1962    Lady Noble dies at No 22
1967    No 1 bought for Bath Preservation Trust by Major Bernard
        Cayzer
1972    Miss Wellesley-Colley wins 'yellow door' case
1976    Shooting of scenes for film 'Joseph Andrews' in Crescent
1979    New Royal Crescent Hotel opens

# The Younger John Wood's Contracting Method

It may be of interest to elaborate a little on the manner in which John Wood the younger conducted his affairs as a speculative builder and an architect, particularly with regard to the Royal Crescent. Firstly, he acquired the land — in this case at an annual rental of £200 per annum — and then disposed of individual plots to builders at a quarterly rental. The builders then erected the houses to his basic plan, keeping strictly to his design for the façades; and finally each builder negotiated a contract with a purchaser, which outlined the various modifications, required by the purchaser, in the interior of the house.

No 7 the Crescent was built by Michael Hemmings, carpenter, of the parish of Walcot. Wood's contract with him is dated 1st January, 1767, and reads as follows:

'Agreed this first day of January one thousand seven hundred and sixty seven, between John Wood of the Parish of Walcot in the County of Somerset, Esquire, and Michael Hemmings of the same Parish, carpenter. That for, and in the same consideration of the sum of Thirteen pounds a year, payable quarterly to the said John Wood and his heirs for ever, clear of all taxes and deductions whatsoever, he, the same John Wood, shall, at the costs of the said Michael Hemmings, convey unto him and his heirs for ever, All that plott, piece or parcel of ground being part of the field commonly called the Hayes Lower Furlong in the said Parish of Walcot, fronting west-wards to an open area called the Royall Crescent . . . and the said Michael Hemmings does agree to build one substantial house at the westward end of the said ground according to the plans of the said John Wood, and will begin the same immediately . . . and will have before the said front a pavement twelve feet wide, and pitch a coach road twenty four feet wide . . . before Midsummer, One thousand seven hundred and sixty eight, the rent of the said ground to com-mence on the twenty fifth day of March, One thousand seven hundred and seventy . . . With a further Covenant to be at a joint expence with the Proprietors of other houses in the said Crescent, to inclose with an iron rail the grass plott in the front of the said Crescent, and to keep the same in repair'.

Hemmings built the house with a purchaser in mind; Mrs Elizabeth Tyndall, a widow, agreed to pay him £1,700 for it, and on the 8th February, 1771 they signed a contract which specified Mrs Tyndall's individual requirements. Here is part of the text:

'. . . And whereas the said Michael Hemmings hath lately erected and built . . . a good, firm and substantial messuage or tenement. And Whereas the said Elizabeth Tyndall hath agreed with the said Michael Hemmings for the purchase of the said messuage or tenement and premises, at and for the price or sum of seventeen hundred pounds . . . it is therefore agreed . . . that the said Michael Hemmings shall and will grant release and convey (to Elizabeth Tyndall) the said several pieces and parcels of ground, messuage or tenement so erected . . . And also that the said Michael Hemmings . . . shall find and provide and also fix up in the following rooms, closets and places of the said messuage, the several matters and things hereinafter taken notice of.'

The modifications required by Mrs Tyndall were then listed. She required a range in the kitchen, a wash house, shelves in the house-keeper's room, and arches in the wine-cellar. A large closet under the stairs was to be fitted with shelves, and a servant's privy was to be installed, 'neatly fitted up'. The hall was to be paved with Portland stone dotted with black marble. A window was to be changed in the store room, and the back parlour, dining-room and other rooms were to be equipped with marble chimney pieces. Steps were to be made down into the front area. And Mrs Tyndall also required Hemmings 'to make a privy in the garden', and to level the ground behind the house 'agreeable to the directions of the gardener immediately'. He was to allow sixpence a yard for paper in all rooms except garrets, 'and to be finished the first day of May in the year of our Lord One thousand seven hundred and seventy one'.

No 7, it may be remembered, belonged to Mrs Rottboll in 1970, and was described then as a splendid house. Many modifications were carried out during its long history, particularly in the Victorian era; but Hemmings' basic structure, and the 'matters and things' that he attended to for Mrs Tyndall, set the standard for its high quality in 1771.

A Note on the Life of John Wood the Younger

When he commenced the building of the Crescent in 1767, the younger John Wood was thirty-nine years old. He was married with seven children — all girls — and he lived at No 41 Gay Street. Two boys, born later, completed the family.

Wood was born on the 25th February, 1728, at Eagle House, Batheaston. The bronze tablet on the Gay Street house gives the year of his birth as 1727, but this is probably due to an equivocal interpretation of the records. Before 1750, the legal year began on 25th March. All documents bearing dates between January and March were usually endorsed with the figures for two consecutive years, to cover the discrepancy between legal and calendar years; thus Wood's birth date was recorded as '25th day of February, 1727/28'.

From a very early age he was assiduously schooled in the principles of architecture by his father. John Wood senior was fascinated by the Druids and their beliefs and customs, and he often visited Stonehenge to survey the site; he even published a book entitled *Choir Gaure, Vulgarly called Stonehenge, on Salisbury Plain, Described, Restored and Explained\**. In 1740 he took his twelve-year-old son to the site, and later described, in a letter, how he tried 'to imprint on the mind of my eldest son and chief assistant, the strongest ideas of accuracy in this, his first practical lesson of surveying'. The young assistant proved to be an excellent pupil; and when, in 1749, Wood senior was commissioned to design a new town hall at Liverpool, the contract specified that young John should accompany his father, and reside in the city during the summer months, until the work was completed.

The new town hall naturally attracted a number of visitors from nearby cities and towns. Among them was Thomas Brock, the town clerk of Chester. He became friendly with the two Woods, and it seems likely that he invited them to his home, Bostock Hall in

---

\*'Choir Gaure' has since been interpreted as 'great' or 'circular' 'temple' or 'gathering place'.

Cheshire. Certainly in the course of the friendship, young John met Brock's sister, Elizabeth, and fell in love with her. They married in 1752; and Wood senior underlined the union of the two families by making Brock his son's trustee.*

This was typical of the older man; he was a dedicated architect and a businessman who had acquired considerable wealth during his career, and in Thomas Brock he saw the ideal financial partner for his son — a successful administrator, a man of means, and a relative by marriage. The younger Wood, brilliant architect though he was, seems to have lacked some of his father's drive and business acumen; he had a social conscience that occasionally clashed with his entrepreneurial ideas, and he probably lacked the touch of ruthlessness that made the elder Wood so materially successful.

He was certainly an amiable man, with a wry sense of humour. Whilst in Liverpool with his father, he heard of an unusual society that had been founded in 1743 by local merchants, ship owners, sea-captains and professional men. It was called 'The Most Honourable and Facetious Society of Ugly Faces', and its rules were most explicit; members were to be bachelors, men of honour, and of a facetious disposition — and each member was to have 'something odd, remarkable, droll, or out of the way in his Phiz'. Wood was admitted to membership on 22nd July, 1751, after describing his qualifications as 'A stone-coloured complexion, a dimple in his attic story, the Pillasters of his face fluted, tortoise-eyed, a prominent nose. Wild grin, and face altogether resembling a badger, and finer though smaller than Sir Chris Wren or Inego Jones's'.

Wood senior, one feels, would have been horrified at such pointless frivolity. But his son's membership was not to be a long one. The society's rules specified that when a member married, he automatically resigned, and forfeited 'ten shillings and six pence for the use of the Society'; and the accounts contain a revealing item dated 25th September, 1752: 'To Forfeits — Mr John Wood for Marriage: ten shillings and six pence'. Elizabeth had terminated that little bit of nonsense very effectively indeed.

*Most writers on Bath's history, when discussing the origin of Brock Street, state that Thomas Brock was the younger Wood's father-in-law. The evidence demonstrably contradicts this: he was the brother of Wood's wife, Elizabeth.

After the marriage, they came to Bath and the house in Gay Street. Two years later, Wood senior died, only a few months after laying the foundation stone of the Circus, and young John, now twenty-six, completed his father's great work, and went on to ensure his own immortality with the building of the Crescent and the new Assembly Rooms. Posterity has acknowledged his genius fulsomely. 'The finest achievements of the son surpass those of the father' wrote Ison, 'both in breadth of conception and subtlety of realization. In fact, the work of the younger Wood represents the highest point of the Palladian achievement in Bath'.

Towards the end of his life he was deeply concerned over the poor housing conditions of labourers and artisans. The overcrowding, and the damp, unhealthy nature of most of the ramshackle, unsanitary cottages in which they lived, appalled him; and in 1780 he published *A Series of Plans for Cottages or Habitations of the Labourer, either in Husbandry or the Mechanic's Arts*' in which he undoubtedly staked a claim to be the first social reformer in architecture. Many of his stipulations, now two hundred years old, would find endorsement today. Floors, he insisted, should be sixteen inches to eighteen inches above ground level, and rooms should be at least eight feet high. Stone walls should be sixteen inches thick, and cottages should be built, not singly, but in pairs 'for mutual assistance in case of illness'. Each one should have a garden, and should never be far from a well or spring; and there should be one bedroom for parents, and one each for boys and girls.

All this was a far cry from the opulence of the Royal Crescent, but it emphasises Wood's awareness of his social obligations as an architect. He was never as wealthy as his father, but his heart, as they say, was in the right place. Although the Crescent, brilliantly conceived and executed, remains his lasting memorial, it is worth remembering him, too, as a compassionate and very humane man.

He died in 1801, and was buried in the chancel of Swainswick church, next to the grave of his father. Elizabeth lived on into the nineteenth century. In 1807 she was living in an impoverished state at Richmond in Surrey, and appealed to Bath Corporation for financial help. She was granted a pension of twenty pounds a year for the remainder of her life, in view of the distinguished services rendered by her husband to the city.

# A Select Bibliography

Baker, A. *The Life of Sir Isaac Pitman* 1913
Barbeau, A. *Life and Letters at Bath in the Eighteenth Century* 1904
Blunt, R. (ed) *Mrs Montagu, 'Queen of the Blues'; her Letters and Friendships* 2 vols 1923
Burney, F. *Journals and Letters of Fanny Burney* 1972
Cobbe, F. P. *The Life of Frances Power Cobbe* 1904
Cronin, V. *Louis and Antoinette* 1974
Freeman, J. *Jane Austen in Bath* 1969
Fulford, R. *Royal Dukes* 1933
Gadd, D. *Georgian Summer* 1972
Gosse, P. *Dr Viper (Biography of Philip Thicknesse)* 1952
Green, M. A. *The Eighteenth Century Architecture of Bath* 1904
Haddon, J. *Bath* 1973
Hare, A. J. C. *The Story of My Life* 6 vols 1896–1900
Ison, W. *The Georgian Buildings of Bath* 1970
Little, B. *Bath Portrait* 1968
Little, B. *The Building of Bath* 1947
Mainwaring, R. *Annals of Bath* 1838
Meehan, J. F. *Famous Houses of Bath* 1901
Montagu, Mrs E. *Letters* 4 vols 1810–1813
Peach, R. E. M. *Historic Houses in Bath* 1883
Robertson, C. *Bath: an Architectural Guide* 1975
Tegg, T. *Memoirs of Sir Francis Burdett* n.d.
Thicknesse, P. *Memoirs and anecdotes* 1788
Thicknesse, P. *New Prose Bath Guide* 1778
Trevelyan, G. M. *English Social History* 1944
Tyte, W. *Bath in the Eighteenth Century* 1903
Warner, R. *The History of Bath* 1801
Whalley, T. S. *Journals and Correspondence* 2 vols. 1863
White, T. H. *The Age of Scandal* 1950
— and contemporary newspapers and directories, guides, pamphlets. and articles in journals.

# Index

# Index

# Index

# Index